BREAD MACHINE COOKBOOK

Mastering the Art of Baking with Easy, Delicious Recipes and Tips for Fresh Homemade Bread

THALIA .S. CALDWELL

Copyright © 2024 By **THALIA .S. CALDWELL**. All rights reserved worldwide.

No part of this book may be reproduced or transmitted in any form or by any means, electronic or mechanical, including photocopying, recording, or by any information storage and retrieval system, without written permission from the publisher, except for the inclusion of brief quotations in a review.

WarningDisclaimer:

The purpose of this book is to educate and entertain. The author or publisher does not guarantee that anyone following the techniques, suggestions, tips, ideas, or strategies will become successful. The author and publisher shall have neither liability nor responsibility to anyone with respect to any loss or damage caused, or alleged to be caused, directly or indirectly, by the information contained in this book.

This copyright notice and disclaimer apply to the entirety of the book and its contents, whether in print or electronic form, and extend to all future editions or revisions of the book. Unauthorized use or reproduction of this book or its contents is strictly prohibited and may result in legal action.

INTRODUCTION 8
Overview of bread machines: 9
Essential ingredients and tools for successful bread making: 10

CHAPTER ONE: GETTING STARTED WITH BREAD MACHINE BASICS 12
Bread Machine Settings and Functions 13
Understanding Different Types of Flours 15
Yeast and Rising Techniques 16

CHAPTER TWO: CLASSIC BREAD LOAVES 18
Classic White Bread 18
Classic Whole Wheat Bread 18
Classic Honey Oat Bread 19
Classic Italian Herb Bread 20
Classic Rye Bread 20
Classic Potato Bread 21
Classic Milk Bread 22
Classic Multigrain Bread 22
Classic Cheese Bread 23
Classic Garlic Bread 24
Classic Onion Bread 24
Classic Brioche 25
Classic Challah 26
Classic Ciabatta 27
Classic Focaccia 28
Classic Baguettes 29
Classic Sourdough Bread 30
Classic Pumpernickel Bread 30

CHAPTER THREE: SWEET BREADS AND ROLLS 32
Perfect Cinnamon Rolls 32
Sticky Caramel Pecan Buns 33
Irresistible Monkey Bread 34
Homemade Hawaiian Rolls 35
Golden Dinner Rolls 36
Buttery Parker House Rolls 37
Fluffy Cloverleaf Rolls 38
Homemade Crescent Rolls 39

Buttery Brioche Rolls 40
Raisin Bread Delight 41
Cinnamon Swirl Bread 42
Luscious Lemon Bread 43
Orange Zest Bread... 43
Banana Bliss Bread 44
Zucchini Harvest Bread 45
Autumn Pumpkin Bread 46
Cranberry Orange Bread 47
Chocolate Chip Banana Bread 48

CHAPTER FOUR: FLATBREADS AND PIZZAS 49

Perfect Pizza Dough... 49
Herb Focaccia 50
Garlic Naan 51
Pita Bread 52
Tortillas 52
Chapati... 53
Calzone Dough 54
Stromboli... 55
Bagels 56
English Muffins 57
Pretzels.. 58
Breadsticks 59
Crackers 60
Lavash 61
Pita Chips 62
Tortilla Chips 63
Herb Bread 64
Garlic Knots 64

CHAPTER FIVE: GLUTENFREE AND SPECIALTY BREADS.....................................66

GlutenFree Bread 66
Keto Bread 67
Paleo Bread 67
Vegan Bread.. 68
NutFree Bread 69
DairyFree Bread 70

LowCarb Bread 70
HighProtein Bread 71
Sprouted Grain Bread 72
Quinoa Bread 73
Cornbread 73
Biscuits 74
Scones 75
Muffins 76
Bagels 77
Tortillas 78
English Muffins 79
Flatbread 80

CHAPTER SIX: BREADS WITH MIXINS 81

Cheese Bread 81
Herb Bread 82
Olive Bread 82
Garlic Bread 83
Onion Bread 84
Bacon Bread 85
Jalapeno Bread 85
Dried Fruit Bread 86
Walnut Bread 87
Cranberry Bread 88
Cheddar Bread 89
Feta Bread 89
Sundried Tomato Bread 90
Rosemary Bread 91
Pesto Bread 92
Spinach Bread 92
Caramelized Onion Bread 93
Raisin Bread 94

CHAPTER SEVEN: ARTISAN BREADS 95

Sourdough Bread 95
Ciabatta 96
Focaccia 97
Baguettes 98

Batards.. 99
Boules 99
Rye Bread 100
Pumpernickel Bread 101
Multigrain Bread 102
Semmel Rolls 102
Pretzels... 103
Bagels 104
English Muffins 105
Croissants... 106
Brioche 107
Challah 108
Pain au Lait 109
Pain de Campagne 110

CHAPTER EIGHT: INTERNATIONAL BREAD 111

French Bread 111
Italian Bread... 111
German Bread 112
Greek Bread 113
Middle Eastern Bread 114
Indian Naan.. 114
Mexican Bolillos 115
Japanese Milk Bread 116
Chinese Steamed Buns 117
Swedish Limpa.. 118
Russian Rye Bread 119
Polish Babka... 120
Irish Soda Bread 121
Portuguese Sweet Bread 122
Cuban Bread... 123
Brazilian Cheese Bread 123
Moroccan Khobz... 124
Turkish Pide 125

CHAPTER NINE: BREAD MACHINE DOUGHS 127

Perfect Pizza Dough.. 127
Calzone Dough 128

Stromboli Dough *129*
Classic Cinnamon Roll Dough *130*
Pretzel Dough... *131*
Homemade Bagel Dough... *132*
English Muffin Dough *133*
Buttery Croissant Dough *134*
Danish Dough... *135*
Puff Pastry Dough *136*
Pie Crust Dough.. *137*
Breadstick Dough *138*
Tortilla Dough *138*
Naan Dough *139*
Pita Dough *140*
Flatbread Dough *141*
Donut Dough *142*
Fritter Dough.. *143*
CONCLUSION 144

INTRODUCTION

Bread has been a staple food for centuries across cultures, providing a convenient, portable, and nourishing way to enjoy grains. However, the traditional process of making bread entirely from scratch at home has often been laborious and timeconsuming requiring precise measuring, extended periods of kneading, and vigilant monitoring to ensure the proper rise and bake. That's where the humble yet ingenious bread machine comes in, revolutionizing how even novice bakers can easily produce fresh, delectable loaves with consistent results.

A bread machine is a compact countertop appliance designed to automate nearly every step of the breadmaking process from start to finish. These machines take the guesswork and effort out of mixing, kneading, rising, and baking dough, allowing you to enjoy homemade bread with minimal handson time and expertise required. While the basic ingredients are still necessary, the machine does all the hard work for you.

The process is refreshingly simple: measure out the required flour, yeast, liquids, salt, sweeteners, fats, and any other additions for your desired recipe, then layer them into the nonstick bread pan in the proper order. Make a few setting selections on the control panel for the bread type, crust color, and loaf size, then press start and let the machine work its magic. You can even set a delay timer so your fresh loaf is ready whenever you'd like it.

As the cycle begins, an electric motor spins a kneading paddle through the dough at timed intervals, developing those crucial gluten strands that will give your bread an artisan bakerystyle chewiness and structure. The heating elements in the small oven chamber surrounding the bread pan provide the perfect temperaturecontrolled environment for the dough to rise slowly and evenly. Most models include a viewing window so you can watch this culinary alchemy in action right on your countertop.

When the baking cycle completes in just a few hours, a hot, fresh loaf emerges piping, fragrant, and ready to slice and enjoy with just a fraction of the effort required for traditional handbaked bread. Many machines even keep the finished loaf in a warm setting for an hour or more until you're ready to partake.

Beyond basic breads, many versatile bread maker models today offer a range of preprogrammed cycles for specialties like whole wheat, glutenfree, sweet breads, doughs for pasta or pizza, and even jam or cake batter. Higherend machines allow you to fully customize your own baking cycles with infinite creativity. But even the most basic model takes the guesswork and effort out of baking fresh loaves at home daily.

For both seasoned bakers and novices alike, the bread machine provides a gateway to the unparalleled taste of homemade bread baked to perfection with the convenience of modern automation. In the following sections, we'll guide you through choosing the ideal machine for your needs and understanding the key ingredients and tools for consistent breadbaking success.

Overview of bread machines:

At its core, a bread machine is an ingeniously simple yet powerful appliance designed to automate nearly every aspect of the breadbaking process. While seemingly modest in appearance as a compact countertop device, these machines pack an array of integrated features that replicate the laborintensive tasks of a professional baker with consistently delicious results.

The primary component is the nonstick bread pan that fits securely into the small oven chamber. This pan typically includes one or more detachable kneading paddles connected to a rotating shaft. As the baking cycle begins, an electric motor precisely controls the rotation of these paddles through the dough at programmed intervals. This controlled kneading action develops and strengthens the gluten strands that provide the ideal chewy texture and structure to the finished loaf.

Surrounding this central bread pan is the heating element and oven chamber itself. By automatically adjusting the temperature at key points in the baking cycle, the chamber creates the optimal environment for the dough to rise slowly and evenly through its initial cool proofing period. As the cycle progresses, the heat is increased in stages to lock in that perfectly baked loaf with a browned, crisped crust encasing a tender, lightasair interior.

While this interplay between synchronized kneading and timed baking temperatures is happening automatically, most modern bread machines also include viewing windows so you can watch the entire magical process unfold. As the dough balls up and spins during its initial kneading phase, stretching and developing those gluten strands, you can observe it expanding in size during the rise. The aroma of freshly baking bread will begin wafting through your kitchen as the browned crust forms in the final stages.

In addition to this core baking automation, many bread makers include convenience features that make the whole process seamless from start to finish. Delay timers allow you to load ingredients in advance and have a freshly baked loaf ready exactly when you'd like it – whether for breakfast, after work, or anytime. Audible tones indicate when to add nutrientpacked ingredients like nuts, seeds, dried fruits, or herbs midcycle without interfering with the kneading or rise.

Most models provide multiple bread settings to choose from so you can produce rustic artisanstyle loaves just as easily as buttermilk bread or glutenfree options. With a userfriendly control panel, you simply select the desired bread type and your preferred crust shade, then let the machine do the rest. Some models even allow you to intervene and remove the dough after its final rise if you'd prefer to bake it in a conventional oven for a crisper, more rustic crust.

Once the baking cycle is complete, many bread makers will automatically switch to a warming mode that keeps your fresh loaf at an ideal serving temperature for up to an hour or more if you aren't ready to enjoy it immediately. With this simple, handsoff automation handling every aspect of the process, you can experience the unbeatable taste and aroma of homemade bread with a tiny fraction of the effort required for traditional hand baking.

Essential ingredients and tools for successful bread making:

While a bread machine does the hard work of mixing, kneading, rising and baking for you, understanding the core ingredients that go into creating deliciously fresh loaves is still key to achieving optimal results. Just like a master baker needs to combine the right components in precise ways, setting yourself up with the proper ingredients and basic tools will ensure consistent breadbaking success with your new appliance.

Let's start with the essential ingredients that form the foundation of any good bread dough:

Flour This is the main structural ingredient providing the bulk and framework for your loaf. While allpurpose flour can work in a pinch, bread flour containing a higher protein content is ideal for better rise, chewier texture, and overall bread quality. Experiment with different grain varieties like whole wheat or nut flours for distinct flavors.

Yeast This leavening powerhouse is responsible for the dough rise by producing carbon dioxide through fermentation. For best results, use active dry yeast or quickrise yeast formulated specifically for bread machines. Always check yeast packet expiration dates and proof it if you're ever unsure of its condition.

Liquids Water, milk, or plantbased milk alternatives provide the moisture needed to activate the yeast and bind the dough together. Following recipe temperatures precisely is crucial too hot will kill the yeast while too cold will impede its ability to rise properly.

Salt While often overlooked, salt plays a vital role in enhancing flavors and tenderizing dough texture. Use appropriate amounts as specified since too little will yield dry, lackluster bread and too much can inhibit the yeast from rising adequately.

Fats/Enrichments For extra tender, flavorful loaves, add enrichments like eggs, butter, olive oil, milk powder, or honey. These ingredients create softer interior textures and help extend the freshness of your finished bread.

With those core ingredients on hand and properly measured, you'll also need a few basic tools and techniques to streamline your breadmaking process:

Measuring Cups/Spoons For accuracy and consistent results, use proper dry and liquid measuring utensils rather than estimating. Spoon dry ingredients into cups instead of scooping compacted amounts.

Thermometer Monitoring liquid temperatures precisely is crucial for activating yeast properly. An instantread thermometer takes the guesswork out of this key step.

Bread Lame This razor tool allows you to score decorative patterns on top of dough for an artisan, bakerystyle finish on your loaves.

Oven Mitts Bread pans get extremely hot during the baking cycle. Wear oven mitts or pads to safely remove the scalding pan when your fresh loaf is ready.

Following your machine's instructions for adding ingredients in the proper order is also important. Typically, you'll add wet components like water or milk first, followed by dry ingredients with the yeast going in very last to avoid activating it prematurely.

With a wellstocked pantry of quality breadmaking essentials combined with these simple tools and tips, you'll have all the components needed to create fresh, bakeryworthy loaves from the comfort of your own kitchen. In the next chapter, we'll guide you through getting started with your machine's cycles and settings for your first baked masterpiece!

CHAPTER ONE: GETTING STARTED WITH BREAD MACHINE BASICS

With your new bread machine unpacked and knowledge of the key ingredients under your belt, it's time to start exploring how to actually operate this marvelous appliance. While specific models may differ slightly, most bread makers share some core settings and functions that are important to understand from the outset.

Let's start with the control panel this is where you'll select which cycle or bread type you want to prepare. Higherend models offer an extensive range of specialized options like glutenfree, artisan, sweet bread, doughonly for pasta or pizza, and more. But even basic machines will have preset cycles for popular varieties like whole wheat, French bread, rapid bake, and others.

Specialty cycles aside, you'll typically need to make a few standard selections no matter which type of loaf you want:

Crust Shade This setting allows you to specify your desired crust color from light to dark based on baking time adjustments. Those who love a thick, crunchy exterior will opt for a darker shade while others may prefer a softer, gently browned crust.

Loaf Size Most modes provide a choice between at least two or three different loaf size capacities, commonly 1 lb, 1.5 lbs, or up to 2.5 lbs. Smaller loaves require less baking time but also use fewer ingredients overall for just 12 servings. Larger ones are great for bigger households.

Delay Timer One of the most convenient bread machine features is the delay timer which allows you to load ingredients and program the full bake cycle to start hours later. Wake up to fresh bread in the morning or have it ready when you want by setting this ahead of time.

As the baking cycle begins, your machine will first mix and knead the dough ingredients for a preliminary stage. This initial kneading develops the gluten structure that provides loft and chewiness. The dough then gets its first rise as the yeast activates and fermentation occurs.

After that first rise period, there is typically a second more brief knead followed by the final rise before the baking phase begins. It's during that second kneading stage that you'll often hear a signal beep, alerting you to quickly lift the lid and add in any desired mixins like nuts, raisins, herbs, or other extras you want incorporated into your loaf.

From there, the bake cycle takes over with regulated heating to transform the risen dough into a glorious, fragrant loaf with that perfect crumb texture sealed inside a browned crust. Most models automatically go into a keep warm mode after baking completes so you can grab and enjoy the loaf whenever you're ready.

With a basic understanding of those core functions and cycles, you're ready to start using your machine for simple batch loaves, taking mental notes on any additional settings to explore further. The instruction manual is a great way to get acquainted with all the features and preprogrammed options specific to your model. After just a few practice loaves, operating your bread maker will become an easy, satisfying routine for fresh homemade bread daily.

In the next sections, we'll dive into key tips on ingredients like various flours and working with yeast for optimal rising and texture in your baked creations. With those fundamental insights, you'll be a bread machine master in no time!

Bread Machine Settings and Functions

At first glance, the control panel of your new bread machine may look intimidating with its array of settings and functions. But don't worry while modern models offer an impressive level of programmability, the core settings are relatively straightforward to understand. Taking a few minutes to get acquainted with what each one does will help you navigate your machine like a pro right from the start.

Let's begin with the main cycle or menu setting. This is where you select which category or type of bread you want to make basic, French, whole wheat, glutenfree, sweet bread, doughonly for pasta or pizza, and so on. Higherend models expand these options even further with cycles for artisan loaves, jam, cake, or custom baking. But even basic machines will have presets for all the most popular styles.

No matter which cycle you choose, you'll typically need to specify a few basic parameters:

Crust Shade This setting adjusts the intensity and duration of the bake phase to produce a light, medium, or dark crust color. Those who love a thick, crunchy crust will go for the darker shade while others may prefer a soft, delicate browning.

Loaf Size Most cycles give you two or three loaf size capacities to choose from, such as 1 lb, 1.5 lbs, or up to 2 lbs. As you can expect, smaller loaves use less overall dough and bake slightly faster while larger ones take more time and ingredients for bigger portions.

MixIn Signal During the second knead cycle, many machines will sound an audible beep to alert you to quickly lift the lid and toss in any desired mixin ingredients like nuts, dried fruits, herbs, or other extras to get them fully incorporated into the dough.

Once you've selected the cycle type and configured those basic settings, you may have additional options depending on your machine's capabilities.

Delay Timer This extremely convenient feature allows you to load all ingredients ahead of time and program the full bake cycle to automatically start hours later perfect for waking up to fresh bread in the morning.

Custom Programming Some higherend models let you override the preset cycles to create fully customized bake, knead, rise, and timing sequences for specialized loaves or experimentation.

Extra Functions Other bread makers include special modes for ultrafast baking, artisanstyle baking with a crisper crust, jam or compote cycles, doughonly kneading for pasta or pizza crust, and more.

Once you start the bake process, most machines will handle all the kneading, rising, and baking automatically according to the selected program settings. The ingredients transform from a rough dough to a smooth, risen ball before baking into a perfect goldenbrown loaf.

Many units even have an automatic keep warm mode to prevent your fresh loaf from cooling down until you're ready to enjoy it. With the core functions figured out, you can start exploring your model's specialty settings or get creative designing your own custom baking sequences.

In just a few bakes, simply selecting your desired loaf type and configuring those initial settings will become an easy, satisfying routine for homemade bread perfection every time. The machine does all the hard work you just sit back and enjoy those incredible freshbaked aromas!

Understanding Different Types of Flours

At the very foundation of any good bread recipe is flour the core ingredient that provides the structural backbone for your final loaf. While you can certainly use basic allpurpose flour for most bread machine recipes, understanding the distinct properties and nuances of different flour varieties allows you to truly take your baking to the next level.

Let's start with the flour that is considered the gold standard for superior bread baking:

Bread Flour This highprotein flour contains more gluten than allpurpose, typically 1214% protein compared to 1012% for AP. Those extra gluten strands are what give bread its characteristic chew and allows loaves to rise higher with better structural integrity. The result is bread with an artisanstyle irregular crumb and lofty, chewy texture. Bread flour is ideal for crusty loaves like French or Italian.

AllPurpose Flour As the name implies, AP flour can be used for just about anything but it may not produce quite as delicious a loaf as bread flour. With its lower protein content, allpurpose allows less gluten development which yields a smaller rise and tighter crumb structure. The finished loaf may be a bit more dense and dry as a result.

Whole Wheat Flour By maintaining the full robust wheat kernel intact, this flour option packs extra nutrition from the wheat germ and bran alongside the endosperm. It creates heartier, nuttiertasting loaves but if used exclusively can result in overly dense, dry texture since the bran cuts down on gluten development and moistness.

GlutenFree Flour Blends For those who cannot consume gluten, there are many alternative glutenfree flour blends made from combinations of rice flour, tapioca flour, corn flour, nut flours, and other nonwheat bases. Since these lack gluten's elastic structure, eggs, xanthan gum, or other binders are typically used to help the dough rise and set properly.

Specialty Flours To create distinctive flavors and nutrition profiles, you can experiment with incorporating small portions of other flour varieties like ancient grains (amaranth, quinoa, millet), nut flours, corn flour, oat flour, rye flour, or chickpea flour among others. Used in moderation to complement rather than replace standard wheat flours, these can make uniquely delicious loaves.

No matter which type of flour you use as your base, it's important to follow recipe instructions closely and make only modest substitutions at first until you understand how different flours behave. Dramatically changing flour varieties often requires adjusting other ingredients like liquids, leavening, salt, and fats to compensate.

The good news is that bread machines allow you to test and learn about various flours easily. Start with recipes calling for one type, then experiment by incorporating small amounts of other flours for flavor and texture variations. With some practice baking under your belt, you'll quickly get a feel for which flours or custom flour blends produce your preferred style of fresh loaf.

In the next section, we'll explore the crucial role of yeast in the breadmaking process and provide some handy tips for ensuring optimal rising capabilities in your bread machine bakes.

Yeast and Rising Techniques

While flour provides the foundational structure, it's the humble yet mighty leavening power of yeast that transforms a dense dough into a light, airy loaf of bread through fermentation. Bakers have spent centuries experimenting with techniques to coax the best rising potential out of this microscopic ingredient. With a bread machine, much of that effort is handled automatically but understanding some yeast basics will help you consistently achieve superior rise and texture.

Let's start with the different yeast varieties suitable for bread:

Active Dry Yeast This is the most common variety found in grocery stores. The dormant but living yeast cells need to be dissolved in warm liquid (105°F115°F) before using to reactivate and kickstart the fermentation process. Many standard bread recipes specify this type.

Bread Machine or Rapid/QuickRise Yeast Formulated with finer granules and more potent dough conditioners, this variety can activate more rapidly without being proofed first. It accelerates overall rise times, ideal for express bread maker cycles.

Fresh Cake Yeast While not as convenient as dry yeasts, this perishable soft cube provides leavening power desirable for authentically rustic, artisanstyle breads. Typically used by professional bakers.

Regardless of type, always check that your yeast isn't past its expiration or "Best If Used By" date. Many bakers do a simple proofing test by dissolving the yeast in some warm water with a pinch of sugar to ensure it's still nice and active before baking.

So once that yeast is ready to go, how exactly does it create those perfect air pockets in our loaves? Through fermentation a process where the yeast consumes the sugars and starches present in the dough while releasing carbon dioxide gas as a byproduct. These gas bubbles allow the dough to rise and develop an airy, lofty interior texture.

Temperature regulation is crucial here. Excessive heat over 120°F will kill the yeast entirely, while cooler temps below 70°F won't provide enough warmth to activate and accelerate the yeast's work. Most recipes call for a draftfree environment around 75°F85°F for optimal rising conditions.

Bread machines are perfectly calibrated to automate this proofing process. After that initial mixing of ingredients and kneading to develop gluten structure, the machine goes into its first rise cycle where the dough rests and the yeast goes to work fermenting. A second shorter knead redistributes any escaped gas before the machine enters its final, longer rise period where the dough fully expands to its maximum volume. Then it's showtime for the allimportant bake phase!

The amount of yeast specified in a recipe accounts for factors like dough size, rise times, and baking duration to achieve just the right degree of rising. Too much yeast and the dough can overproof and collapse; too little won't provide enough leavening power to create that coveted open crumb.

By starting with quality yeast at its recommended amount for the type of bread and dough size you're making, combined with precisely calibrated rise periods and temperatures, your bread machine will handle all those critical rising factors automatically. Let the amazing science of fermentation work its magic for you!

CHAPTER TWO: CLASSIC BREAD LOAVES

Classic White Bread

Prep: 10 mins | Cook: 3 hours | Serves: 1 loaf

Ingredients:
US: 1 cup water, 2 tablespoons butter, 3 cups bread flour, 2 tablespoons sugar, 1 1/2 teaspoons salt, 2 1/4 teaspoons active dry yeast

UK: 240ml water, 28g butter, 360g bread flour, 25g sugar, 8g salt, 7g active dry yeast

Instructions:
1. Add water, butter, bread flour, sugar, salt, and yeast to the bread machine pan in the order recommended by the manufacturer.
2. Select the Basic or White Bread setting and start the machine.
3. Once the cycle is complete, remove the bread from the machine and let it cool before slicing.

Nutritional Info: Calories: 150 | Fat: 3g | Carbs: 26g | Protein: 4g

Bread Machine Function: Basic or White Bread Setting

Classic Whole Wheat Bread

Prep: 15 mins | Cook: 3 hours | Serves: 1 loaf

Ingredients:
- **US:** 1 cup water, 2 tablespoons honey, 1 tablespoon olive oil, 2 1/2 cups whole wheat flour, 1 cup bread flour, 1 1/2 teaspoons salt, 2 1/4 teaspoons active dry yeast
- **UK:** 240ml water, 30g honey, 15ml olive oil, 300g whole wheat flour, 130g bread flour, 8g salt, 7g active dry yeast

Instructions:
1. Add water, honey, olive oil, whole wheat flour, bread flour, salt, and yeast to the bread machine pan.
2. Select the Whole Wheat setting and start the machine.
3. Once the cycle is complete, remove the bread from the machine and let it cool before slicing.

Nutritional Info: Calories: 180 | Fat: 2g | Carbs: 35g | Protein: 6g

Bread Machine Function: Whole Wheat Setting

Classic Honey Oat Bread

Prep: 15 mins | Cook: 3 hours | Serves: 1 loaf

Ingredients:
- **US:** 1 cup warm milk, 2 tablespoons honey, 2 tablespoons butter, 1 cup oldfashioned oats, 2 1/2 cups bread flour, 1 1/2 teaspoons salt, 2 1/4 teaspoons active dry yeast
- **UK:** 240ml warm milk, 30g honey, 28g butter, 90g oldfashioned oats, 300g bread flour, 8g salt, 7g active dry yeast

Instructions:
1. Add warm milk, honey, butter, oats, bread flour, salt, and yeast to the bread machine pan.
2. Select the Sweet or Basic setting and start the machine.
3. Once the cycle is complete, remove the bread from the machine and let it cool before slicing.

Nutritional Info: Calories: 200 | Fat: 4g | Carbs: 36g | Protein: 6g

Bread Machine Function: Sweet or Basic Setting

Classic Italian Herb Bread

Prep: 10 mins | Cook: 3 hours | Serves: 1 loaf

Ingredients:
- **US:** 1 cup water, 2 tablespoons olive oil, 3 cups bread flour, 2 tablespoons dried Italian herbs (such as basil, oregano, thyme), 1 1/2 teaspoons salt, 2 1/4 teaspoons active dry yeast
- **UK:** 240ml water, 30ml olive oil, 360g bread flour, 8g dried Italian herbs (such as basil, oregano, thyme), 8g salt, 7g active dry yeast

Instructions:
1. Add water, olive oil, bread flour, Italian herbs, salt, and yeast to the bread machine pan.
2. Select the Basic or Italian Bread setting and start the machine.
3. Once the cycle is complete, remove the bread from the machine and let it cool before slicing.

Nutritional Info: Calories: 180 | Fat: 3g | Carbs: 32g | Protein: 5g

Bread Machine Function: Basic or Italian Bread Setting

Classic Rye Bread

Prep: 10 mins | Cook: 3 hours | Serves: 1 loaf

Ingredients:
- **US:** 1 cup water, 2 tablespoons molasses, 2 tablespoons vegetable oil, 1 1/2 cups rye flour, 1 1/2 cups bread flour, 1 1/2 teaspoons salt, 2 1/4 teaspoons active dry yeast
- **UK:** 240ml water, 30g molasses, 30ml vegetable oil, 180g rye flour, 180g bread flour, 8g salt, 7g active dry yeast

Instructions:
1. Add water, molasses, vegetable oil, rye flour, bread flour, salt, and yeast to the bread machine pan.
2. Select the Rye or Basic setting and start the machine.
3. Once the cycle is complete, remove the bread from the machine and let it cool before slicing.

Nutritional Info: Calories: 200 | Fat: 3g | Carbs: 38g | Protein: 5g

Bread Machine Function: Rye or Basic Setting

Classic Potato Bread

Prep: 15 mins | Cook: 3 hours | Serves: 1 loaf

Ingredients:
- **US:** 1 cup mashed potatoes (cooled), 1/2 cup warm milk, 2 tablespoons butter, 3 cups bread flour, 1 1/2 teaspoons salt, 2 1/4 teaspoons active dry yeast
- **UK:** 240g mashed potatoes (cooled), 120ml warm milk, 28g butter, 360g bread flour, 8g salt, 7g active dry yeast

Instructions:
1. Add mashed potatoes, warm milk, butter, bread flour, salt, and yeast to the bread machine pan.
2. Select the Basic or Potato Bread setting and start the machine.
3. Once the cycle is complete, remove the bread from the machine and let it cool before slicing.

Nutritional Info: Calories: 180 | Fat: 3g | Carbs: 32g | Protein: 5g

Bread Machine Function: Basic or Potato Bread Setting

Classic Milk Bread

Prep: 10 mins | Cook: 3 hours | Serves: 1 loaf

Ingredients:

US: 1 cup warm milk, 2 tablespoons unsalted butter, 3 cups bread flour, 2 tablespoons sugar, 1 1/2 teaspoons salt, 2 1/4 teaspoons active dry yeast

- **UK:** 240ml warm milk, 30g unsalted butter, 360g bread flour, 24g sugar, 8g salt, 7g active dry yeast

Instructions:

1. Add warm milk, unsalted butter, bread flour, sugar, salt, and yeast to the bread machine pan.
2. Select the Basic or Milk Bread setting and start the machine.
3. Once the cycle is complete, remove the bread from the machine and let it cool before slicing.

Nutritional Info: Calories: 190 | Fat: 4g | Carbs: 32g | Protein: 5g

Bread Machine Function: Basic or Milk Bread Setting

Classic Multigrain Bread

Prep: 10 mins | Cook: 3 hours | Serves: 1 loaf

Ingredients:

- **US:** 1 cup water, 2 tablespoons honey, 2 tablespoons vegetable oil, 1 cup whole wheat flour, 2 cups bread flour, 1/2 cup rolled oats, 2 tablespoons flaxseeds, 1 1/2 teaspoons salt, 2 1/4 teaspoons active dry yeast
- **UK:** 240ml water, 30g honey, 30ml vegetable oil, 120g whole wheat flour, 240g bread flour, 60g rolled oats, 30g flaxseeds, 8g salt, 7g active dry yeast

Instructions:
1. Add water, honey, vegetable oil, whole wheat flour, bread flour, rolled oats, flaxseeds, salt, and yeast to the bread machine pan.
2. Select the Whole Wheat or Multigrain setting and start the machine.
3. Once the cycle is complete, remove the bread from the machine and let it cool before slicing.

Nutritional Info: Calories: 220 | Fat: 5g | Carbs: 38g | Protein: 6g

Bread Machine Function: Whole Wheat or Multigrain Setting

Classic Cheese Bread

Prep: 10 mins | Cook: 3 hours | Serves: 1 loaf

Ingredients:
- **US:** 1 cup warm water, 2 tablespoons unsalted butter, 3 cups bread flour, 1 1/2 teaspoons salt, 1 cup shredded cheddar cheese, 2 tablespoons grated Parmesan cheese, 2 1/4 teaspoons active dry yeast
- **UK:** 240ml warm water, 30g unsalted butter, 360g bread flour, 8g salt, 120g shredded cheddar cheese, 24g grated Parmesan cheese, 7g active dry yeast

Instructions:
1. Add warm water, unsalted butter, bread flour, salt, shredded cheddar cheese, Parmesan cheese, and yeast to the bread machine pan.
2. Select the Basic or Cheese Bread setting and start the machine.
3. Once the cycle is complete, remove the bread from the machine and let it cool before slicing.

Nutritional Info: Calories: 220 | Fat: 7g | Carbs: 32g | Protein: 8g

Bread Machine Function: Basic or Cheese Bread Setting

Classic Garlic Bread

Prep: 10 mins | Cook: 3 hours | Serves: 1 loaf

Ingredients:
- **US:** 1 cup warm water, 2 tablespoons olive oil, 3 cups bread flour, 2 teaspoons sugar, 1 1/2 teaspoons salt, 4 cloves garlic (minced), 2 1/4 teaspoons active dry yeast
- **UK:** 240ml warm water, 30ml olive oil, 360g bread flour, 10g sugar, 8g salt, 4 cloves garlic (minced), 7g active dry yeast

Instructions:
1. Add warm water, olive oil, bread flour, sugar, salt, minced garlic, and yeast to the bread machine pan.
2. Select the Basic or Italian Bread setting and start the machine.
3. Once the cycle is complete, remove the bread from the machine and let it cool before slicing.

Nutritional Info: Calories: 200 | Fat: 3g | Carbs: 38g | Protein: 6g

Bread Machine Function: Basic or Italian Bread Setting

Classic Onion Bread

Prep: 10 mins | Cook: 3 hours | Serves: 1 loaf

Ingredients:
- **US:** 1 cup warm water, 2 tablespoons olive oil, 3 cups bread flour, 1 1/2 teaspoons salt, 1 medium onion (finely chopped), 2 tablespoons dried minced onion, 2 1/4 teaspoons active dry yeast
- **UK:** 240ml warm water, 30ml olive oil, 360g bread flour, 8g salt, 1 medium onion (finely chopped), 16g dried minced onion, 7g active dry yeast

Instructions:
1. Add warm water, olive oil, bread flour, salt, finely chopped onion, dried minced onion, and yeast to the bread machine pan.
2. Select the Basic or Onion Bread setting and start the machine.
3. Once the cycle is complete, remove the bread from the machine and let it cool before slicing.

Nutritional Info: Calories: 210 | Fat: 4g | Carbs: 39g | Protein: 7g

Bread Machine Function: Basic or Onion Bread Setting

Classic Brioche

Prep: 15 mins | Cook: 3 hours | Serves: 1 loaf

Ingredients:
- **US:** 3/4 cup warm milk, 3 large eggs, 1/4 cup unsalted butter (softened), 3 cups bread flour, 3 tablespoons sugar, 1 1/2 teaspoons salt, 2 1/4 teaspoons active dry yeast
- **UK:** 180ml warm milk, 3 large eggs, 60g unsalted butter (softened), 360g bread flour, 36g sugar, 8g salt, 7g active dry yeast

Instructions:
1. Add warm milk, eggs, softened unsalted butter, bread flour, sugar, salt, and yeast to the bread machine pan.
2. Select the Basic or French Bread setting and start the machine.
3. Once the cycle is complete, remove the brioche from the machine and let it cool before slicing.

Nutritional Info: Calories: 260 | Fat: 8g | Carbs: 38g | Protein: 8g

Bread Machine Function: Basic or French Bread Setting

Classic Challah

Prep: 15 mins | Cook: 3 hours | Serves: 1 loaf

Ingredients:
- **US:** 1/2 cup warm water, 2 large eggs + 1 egg yolk (reserve the white for egg wash), 1/4 cup vegetable oil, 3 cups bread flour, 1/4 cup sugar, 1 1/2 teaspoons salt, 2 1/4 teaspoons active dry yeast, sesame seeds or poppy seeds for topping (optional)
- **UK:** 120ml warm water, 2 large eggs + 1 egg yolk (reserve the white for egg wash), 60ml vegetable oil, 360g bread flour, 50g sugar, 8g salt, 7g active dry yeast, sesame seeds or poppy seeds for topping (optional)

Instructions:
1. In the bread machine pan, combine warm water, 2 eggs + 1 egg yolk, vegetable oil, bread flour, sugar, salt, and yeast.
2. Select the Dough setting and start the machine.
3. Once the dough cycle is complete, remove the dough and divide it into three equal parts. Roll each part into a long rope and braid them together.
4. Place the braided dough on a greased baking sheet, cover, and let it rise for 3045 minutes.
5. Preheat the oven to 350°F (175°C).
6. Brush the risen dough with the reserved egg white and sprinkle with sesame seeds or poppy seeds if desired.
7. Bake for 2530 minutes or until golden brown.
8. Allow the challah to cool before slicing and serving.

Nutritional Info: Calories: 220 | Fat: 8g | Carbs: 32g | Protein: 6g

Bread Machine Function: Dough Setting

Classic Ciabatta

Prep: 15 mins | Cook: 3 hours | Serves: 1 loaf

Ingredients:
- **US:** 1 cup water, 2 tablespoons olive oil, 2 1/2 cups bread flour, 1 teaspoon sugar, 1 1/2 teaspoons salt, 1 1/2 teaspoons active dry yeast
- **UK:** 240ml water, 30ml olive oil, 300g bread flour, 5g sugar, 8g salt, 7g active dry yeast

Instructions:
1. Add water, olive oil, bread flour, sugar, salt, and yeast to the bread machine pan.
2. Select the Dough setting and start the machine.
3. Once the dough cycle is complete, remove the dough and shape it into a rectangle on a lightly floured surface.
4. Cover the dough with a clean kitchen towel and let it rise for about 3045 minutes.
5. Preheat the oven to 425°F (220°C) and place a baking stone or inverted baking sheet in the oven to preheat.
6. Transfer the risen dough to the preheated baking stone or sheet and bake for 2025 minutes until golden brown and crispy.
7. Allow the ciabatta to cool on a wire rack before slicing.

Nutritional Info: Calories: 190 | Fat: 3g | Carbs: 35g | Protein: 6g

Bread Machine Function: Dough Setting

Classic Focaccia

Prep: 15 mins | Cook: 3 hours | Serves: 1 loaf

Ingredients:
- **US:** 1 cup warm water, 2 tablespoons olive oil, 3 cups bread flour, 1 teaspoon sugar, 1 1/2 teaspoons salt, 2 1/4 teaspoons active dry yeast, 2 tablespoons chopped fresh rosemary, coarse sea salt for topping
- **UK:** 240ml warm water, 30ml olive oil, 360g bread flour, 5g sugar, 8g salt, 7g active dry yeast, 2 tablespoons chopped fresh rosemary, coarse sea salt for topping

Instructions:
1. Place warm water, olive oil, bread flour, sugar, salt, and yeast in the bread machine pan.
2. Select the Dough setting and start the machine.
3. Once the dough cycle is complete, remove the dough and press it evenly into a greased baking sheet.
4. Cover the dough with a clean kitchen towel and let it rise for about 3045 minutes.
5. Preheat the oven to 425°F (220°C).
6. After rising, dimple the dough with your fingers and sprinkle chopped rosemary and coarse sea salt over the top.
7. Bake for 2025 minutes until golden brown and crispy.
8. Allow the focaccia to cool slightly before slicing and serving.

Nutritional Info: Calories: 180 | Fat: 4g | Carbs: 32g | Protein: 6g

Bread Machine Function: Dough Setting

Classic Baguettes

Prep: 15 mins | Cook: 3 hours | Serves: 2 baguettes

Ingredients:
- **US:** 1 cup warm water, 2 teaspoons sugar, 1 1/2 teaspoons salt, 3 cups bread flour, 2 1/4 teaspoons active dry yeast, cornmeal for dusting
- **UK:** 240ml warm water, 10g sugar, 8g salt, 360g bread flour, 7g active dry yeast, cornmeal for dusting

Instructions:
1. Add warm water, sugar, salt, bread flour, and yeast to the bread machine pan.
2. Select the Dough setting and start the machine.
3. Once the dough cycle is complete, remove the dough and divide it into two equal portions.
4. Roll each portion into a long baguette shape and place them on a baking sheet dusted with cornmeal.
5. Cover the baguettes with a clean kitchen towel and let them rise for about 3045 minutes.
6. Preheat the oven to 425°F (220°C).
7. Make diagonal slashes on the top of each baguette with a sharp knife.
8. Bake for 2025 minutes until golden brown and hollowsounding when tapped on the bottom.
9. Allow the baguettes to cool on a wire rack before serving.

Nutritional Info: Calories: 160 | Fat: 1g | Carbs: 32g | Protein: 5g

Bread Machine Function: Dough Setting

Classic Sourdough Bread

Prep: 20 mins | Cook: 3 hours | Serves: 1 loaf

Ingredients:
- **US:** 1 cup sourdough starter, 1 1/4 cups warm water, 3 cups bread flour, 1 1/2 teaspoons salt
- **UK:** 240ml sourdough starter, 300ml warm water, 360g bread flour, 8g salt

Instructions:
1. In the bread machine pan, combine sourdough starter, warm water, bread flour, and salt.
2. Select the Basic or White Bread setting and start the machine.
3. Allow the bread machine to complete the full cycle.
4. Once done, carefully remove the loaf from the bread machine and let it cool on a wire rack.

Nutritional Info: Calories: 140 | Fat: 0.5g | Carbs: 28g | Protein: 5g

Bread Machine Function: Basic or White Bread Setting

Classic Pumpernickel Bread

Prep: 15 mins | Cook: 3 hours | Serves: 1 loaf

Ingredients:
- **US:** 1 cup warm water, 2 tablespoons molasses, 2 tablespoons olive oil, 1 1/2 teaspoons salt, 1 cup rye flour, 2 cups bread flour, 2 tablespoons cocoa powder, 1 tablespoon caraway seeds, 2 1/4 teaspoons active dry yeast
- **UK:** 240ml warm water, 30ml molasses, 30ml olive oil, 8g salt, 120g rye flour, 240g bread flour, 15g cocoa powder, 5g caraway seeds, 7g active dry yeast

Instructions:
1. Add warm water, molasses, olive oil, salt, rye flour, bread flour, cocoa powder, caraway seeds, and active dry yeast to the bread machine pan.
2. Select the Basic or Whole Wheat setting and start the machine.
3. Allow the bread machine to complete the full cycle.
4. Once done, remove the loaf from the bread machine and let it cool completely on a wire rack before slicing.

Nutritional Info: Calories: 170 | Fat: 3g | Carbs: 32g | Protein: 5g

Bread Machine Function: Basic or Whole Wheat Setting

CHAPTER THREE: SWEET BREADS AND ROLLS

Perfect Cinnamon Rolls

Prep: 15 mins | Cook: 2 hours | Serves: 12 rolls

Ingredients:
- **US:** 1 cup warm milk, 2 eggs, 1/3 cup margarine, 4 1/2 cups bread flour, 1 teaspoon salt, 1/2 cup white sugar, 2 1/2 teaspoons bread machine yeast, 1 cup brown sugar, 2 1/2 tablespoons ground cinnamon, 1/3 cup butter (softened), 1 1/2 cups confectioners' sugar, 1 tablespoon milk, 1/4 teaspoon vanilla extract
- **UK:** 240ml warm milk, 2 eggs, 75g margarine, 540g bread flour, 5g salt, 100g white sugar, 7g bread machine yeast, 200g brown sugar, 37g ground cinnamon, 75g butter (softened), 180g confectioners' sugar, 15ml milk, 1ml vanilla extract

Instructions:
1. Place warm milk, eggs, margarine, bread flour, salt, white sugar, and yeast in the bread machine pan.
2. Select the Dough setting and start the machine. Let the dough rise until doubled in size, about 1 hour.
3. Punch down the dough and roll it out on a floured surface into a large rectangle.
4. Spread softened butter over the dough and sprinkle evenly with brown sugar and cinnamon.
5. Roll up the dough tightly, starting from the long side. Cut into 12 equalsized rolls.
6. Place the rolls in a greased 9x13 inch baking pan. Cover and let rise until doubled, about 1 hour.
7. Preheat the oven to 350°F (175°C).
8. Bake the rolls in the preheated oven until golden brown, about 2530 minutes.
9. While the rolls are baking, prepare the glaze by mixing confectioners' sugar, milk, and vanilla extract until smooth.
10. Drizzle the glaze over the warm rolls before serving.

Nutritional Info: Calories: 375 | Fat: 9g | Carbs: 68g | Protein: 7g

Bread Machine Function: Dough Setting

Sticky Caramel Pecan Buns

Prep: 20 mins | Cook: 2.5 hours | Serves: 12 buns

Ingredients:
- **US:** 1/2 cup warm milk, 1/4 cup warm water, 1 egg, 1/4 cup butter (softened), 3 cups bread flour, 1/4 cup white sugar, 1 teaspoon salt, 2 teaspoons bread machine yeast, 1/2 cup chopped pecans, 1/2 cup packed brown sugar, 1/4 cup butter, 2 tablespoons light corn syrup
- **UK:** 120ml warm milk, 60ml warm water, 1 egg, 60g butter (softened), 360g bread flour, 50g white sugar, 5g salt, 7g bread machine yeast, 60g chopped pecans, 100g packed brown sugar, 55g butter, 30ml light corn syrup

Instructions:
1. In the bread machine pan, combine warm milk, warm water, egg, softened butter, bread flour, white sugar, salt, and yeast.
2. Select the Dough setting and start the machine. Allow the dough to knead and rise until doubled in size, about 1 hour.
3. While the dough is rising, prepare the caramel sauce by melting butter, brown sugar, and corn syrup in a saucepan until smooth. Pour into a greased 9x13 inch baking pan and sprinkle with chopped pecans.
4. Once the dough has doubled in size, punch it down and roll it out on a floured surface into a rectangle.
5. Spread softened butter over the dough and sprinkle with brown sugar.
6. Roll up the dough tightly, starting from the long side. Cut into 12 equalsized rolls.
7. Place the rolls in the prepared baking pan on top of the caramel sauce and pecans.
8. Cover and let rise until doubled, about 3045 minutes.
9. Preheat the oven to 375°F (190°C).
10. Bake the rolls in the preheated oven for 2530 minutes, until golden brown.
11. Allow the rolls to cool in the pan for 5 minutes, then invert onto a serving platter.

Nutritional Info: Calories: 280 | Fat: 12g | Carbs: 40g | Protein: 5g

Bread Machine Function: Dough Setting

Irresistible Monkey Bread

Prep: 15 mins | Cook: 1 hour | Serves: 8 servings

Ingredients:
- **US:** 1 cup warm milk, 1/4 cup butter (melted), 2 eggs, 4 cups bread flour, 1/4 cup white sugar, 1 teaspoon salt, 2 teaspoons bread machine yeast, 1/2 cup white sugar, 1 tablespoon ground cinnamon, 1/2 cup butter (melted)
- **UK:** 240ml warm milk, 60g butter (melted), 2 eggs, 480g bread flour, 50g white sugar, 5g salt, 7g bread machine yeast, 100g white sugar, 15g ground cinnamon, 115g butter (melted)

Instructions:
1. Add warm milk, melted butter, eggs, bread flour, white sugar, salt, and yeast to the bread machine pan.
2. Select the Dough setting and start the machine. Allow the dough to knead and rise until doubled in size, about 1 hour.
3. In a separate bowl, mix together white sugar and cinnamon. Set aside.
4. Once the dough has risen, punch it down and divide it into small pieces, about the size of a walnut.
5. Roll each piece into a ball, then dip it into the melted butter and roll it in the cinnamonsugar mixture.
6. Place the coated balls into a greased Bundt pan, layering them evenly.
7. Cover the pan with a clean kitchen towel and let the dough rise again for about 30 minutes.
8. Preheat the oven to 350°F (175°C).
9. Bake the monkey bread in the preheated oven for 3035 minutes, until golden brown and cooked through.
10. Allow the monkey bread to cool in the pan for 510 minutes before inverting it onto a serving plate.

Nutritional Info: Calories: 380 | Fat: 16g | Carbs: 53g | Protein: 7g

Bread Machine Function: Dough Setting

Homemade Hawaiian Rolls

Prep: 15 mins | Cook: 2.5 hours | Serves: 12 rolls

Ingredients:
- **US:** 1 cup warm pineapple juice, 1/4 cup butter (softened), 1 egg, 3 cups bread flour, 1/4 cup white sugar, 1 teaspoon salt, 2 teaspoons bread machine yeast
- **UK:** 240ml warm pineapple juice, 60g butter (softened), 1 egg, 360g bread flour, 50g white sugar, 5g salt, 7g bread machine yeast

Instructions:
1. Combine warm pineapple juice, softened butter, egg, bread flour, white sugar, salt, and yeast in the bread machine pan.
2. Select the Dough setting and start the machine. Allow the dough to knead and rise until doubled in size, about 1 hour.
3. Once the dough has risen, punch it down and divide it into 12 equalsized pieces.
4. Shape each piece into a ball and place them in a greased 9x13 inch baking pan, leaving a little space between each roll.
5. Cover the pan with a clean kitchen towel and let the rolls rise again for about 3045 minutes.
6. Preheat the oven to 350°F (175°C).
7. Bake the rolls in the preheated oven for 2025 minutes, until golden brown and cooked through.
8. Remove from the oven and brush the tops of the rolls with melted butter, if desired.
9. Serve warm and enjoy the soft, fluffy texture of these homemade Hawaiian rolls.

Nutritional Info: Calories: 160 | Fat: 4g | Carbs: 26g | Protein: 4g

Bread Machine Function: Dough Setting

Golden Dinner Rolls

Prep: 15 mins | Cook: 25 mins | Serves: 12 rolls

Ingredients:
- **US:** 1 cup warm milk, 1/4 cup butter (softened), 1 egg, 3 cups bread flour, 1/4 cup white sugar, 1 teaspoon salt, 2 teaspoons bread machine yeast
- **UK:** 240ml warm milk, 60g butter (softened), 1 egg, 360g bread flour, 50g white sugar, 5g salt, 7g bread machine yeast

Instructions:
1. Add warm milk, softened butter, egg, bread flour, white sugar, salt, and yeast to the bread machine pan.
2. Select the Dough setting and start the machine. Allow the dough to knead and rise until doubled in size, about 1 hour.
3. Once the dough has risen, punch it down and divide it into 12 equalsized pieces.
4. Shape each piece into a ball and place them in a greased 9x9 inch baking pan, leaving a little space between each roll.
5. Cover the pan with a clean kitchen towel and let the rolls rise again for about 3045 minutes.
6. Preheat the oven to 375°F (190°C).
7. Bake the rolls in the preheated oven for 2025 minutes, until golden brown and cooked through.
8. Remove from the oven and brush the tops of the rolls with melted butter for added flavor and shine.
9. Serve warm alongside your favorite dishes or use them to make delicious sandwiches.

Nutritional Info: Calories: 160 | Fat: 4g | Carbs: 26g | Protein: 4g

Bread Machine Function: Dough Setting

Buttery Parker House Rolls

Prep: 15 mins | Cook: 25 mins | Serves: 12 rolls

Ingredients:
- **US:** 1 cup warm milk, 1/4 cup butter (melted), 1 egg, 3 cups bread flour, 1/4 cup white sugar, 1 teaspoon salt, 2 teaspoons bread machine yeast, extra melted butter for brushing
- **UK:** 240ml warm milk, 60g butter (melted), 1 egg, 360g bread flour, 50g white sugar, 5g salt, 7g bread machine yeast, extra melted butter for brushing

Instructions:
1. Combine warm milk, melted butter, egg, bread flour, white sugar, salt, and yeast in the bread machine pan.
2. Select the Dough setting and start the machine. Allow the dough to knead and rise until doubled in size, about 1 hour.
3. Once the dough has risen, punch it down and divide it into 12 equalsized pieces.
4. Shape each piece into a ball and place them in a greased 9x13 inch baking pan, pressing them slightly to flatten.
5. Cover the pan with a clean kitchen towel and let the rolls rise again for about 3045 minutes.
6. Preheat the oven to 375°F (190°C).
7. Bake the rolls in the preheated oven for 2025 minutes, until golden brown and cooked through.
8. Brush the warm rolls with melted butter as soon as they come out of the oven for a delicious buttery flavor.
9. Serve these buttery Parker House rolls as a delightful accompaniment to any meal or holiday feast.

Nutritional Info: Calories: 170 | Fat: 6g | Carbs: 25g | Protein: 4g

Bread Machine Function: Dough Setting

Fluffy Cloverleaf Rolls

Prep: 15 mins | Cook: 20 mins | Serves: 12 rolls

Ingredients:
- **US:** 1 cup warm milk, 1/4 cup butter (softened), 1 egg, 3 cups bread flour, 1/4 cup white sugar, 1 teaspoon salt, 2 teaspoons bread machine yeast, extra melted butter for brushing
- **UK:** 240ml warm milk, 60g butter (softened), 1 egg, 360g bread flour, 50g white sugar, 5g salt, 7g bread machine yeast, extra melted butter for brushing

Instructions:
1. Place warm milk, softened butter, egg, bread flour, white sugar, salt, and yeast in the bread machine pan.
2. Select the Dough setting and start the machine. Allow the dough to knead and rise until doubled in size, about 1 hour.
3. After rising, punch down the dough and divide it into 36 equalsized pieces.
4. Shape each piece into a ball and place three balls into each cup of a greased muffin tin.
5. Cover the muffin tin with a clean kitchen towel and let the rolls rise again for about 3045 minutes.
6. Preheat the oven to 375°F (190°C).
7. Bake the rolls in the preheated oven for 1520 minutes, or until they are golden brown on top.
8. Remove the rolls from the oven and brush the tops with melted butter for added flavor.
9. Serve these fluffy cloverleaf rolls warm as a delightful addition to any meal or holiday spread.

Nutritional Info: Calories: 120 | Fat: 4g | Carbs: 18g | Protein: 3g

Bread Machine Function: Dough Setting

Homemade Crescent Rolls

Prep: 20 mins | Cook: 15 mins | Serves: 12 rolls

Ingredients:
- **US:** 1 cup warm milk, 1/4 cup butter (melted), 1 egg, 3 cups bread flour, 1/4 cup white sugar, 1 teaspoon salt, 2 teaspoons bread machine yeast, extra melted butter for brushing
- **UK:** 240ml warm milk, 60g butter (melted), 1 egg, 360g bread flour, 50g white sugar, 5g salt, 7g bread machine yeast, extra melted butter for brushing

Instructions:
1. Combine warm milk, melted butter, egg, bread flour, white sugar, salt, and yeast in the bread machine pan.
2. Select the Dough setting and start the machine. Allow the dough to knead and rise until doubled in size, about 1 hour.
3. Once the dough has risen, punch it down and divide it into 12 equalsized pieces.
4. Roll each piece into a crescent shape, starting with the wide end and rolling towards the point.
5. Place the crescent rolls on a greased baking sheet, leaving a little space between each roll.
6. Cover the baking sheet with a clean kitchen towel and let the rolls rise again for about 3045 minutes.
7. Preheat the oven to 375°F (190°C).
8. Bake the rolls in the preheated oven for 1215 minutes, or until they are golden brown and cooked through.
9. Brush the warm crescent rolls with melted butter for a delicious finishing touch.

Nutritional Info: Calories: 150 | Fat: 5g | Carbs: 22g | Protein: 3g

Bread Machine Function: Dough Setting

Buttery Brioche Rolls

Prep: 20 mins | Cook: 25 mins | Serves: 12 rolls

Ingredients:
- **US:** 1/2 cup warm milk, 3 large eggs, 3 cups bread flour, 1/4 cup white sugar, 1 1/2 teaspoons salt, 1 1/2 teaspoons bread machine yeast, 1/2 cup unsalted butter (softened)
- **UK:** 120ml warm milk, 3 large eggs, 360g bread flour, 50g white sugar, 1 1/2 teaspoons salt, 7g bread machine yeast, 115g unsalted butter (softened)

Instructions:
1. In the bread machine pan, combine warm milk, eggs, bread flour, white sugar, salt, and yeast.
2. Select the Dough setting and start the machine. Allow the dough to knead and rise until doubled in size, about 1 to 1.5 hours.
3. Once the dough has risen, add softened butter to the pan and continue kneading until the butter is fully incorporated and the dough is smooth.
4. Divide the dough into 12 equalsized pieces and shape each piece into a ball.
5. Place the dough balls on a greased baking sheet, leaving space between them to expand.
6. Cover the baking sheet with a clean kitchen towel and let the rolls rise again for about 3045 minutes, until they double in size.
7. Preheat the oven to 375°F (190°C).
8. Bake the brioche rolls in the preheated oven for 2025 minutes, or until they are golden brown and sound hollow when tapped on the bottom.
9. Remove from the oven and cool on a wire rack before serving.

Nutritional Info: Calories: 230 | Fat: 10g | Carbs: 28g | Protein: 6g

Bread Machine Function: Dough Setting

Raisin Bread Delight

Prep: 15 mins | Cook: 3 hours | Serves: 1 loaf

Ingredients:
- **US:** 1 cup warm milk, 2 tablespoons butter (softened), 1 egg, 3 cups bread flour, 1/4 cup white sugar, 1 1/2 teaspoons salt, 2 teaspoons bread machine yeast, 3/4 cup raisins
- **UK:** 240ml warm milk, 30g butter (softened), 1 egg, 360g bread flour, 50g white sugar, 1 1/2 teaspoons salt, 7g bread machine yeast, 110g raisins

Instructions:
1. Place warm milk, softened butter, egg, bread flour, white sugar, salt, and yeast in the bread machine pan in the order recommended by the manufacturer.
2. Select the Sweet Bread setting and start the machine. Allow it to knead the dough and complete the first rise cycle.
3. When the machine beeps to signal adding extras, such as raisins, add them to the dough.
4. Let the bread machine complete the remaining cycles, including the final rise and bake.
5. Once the bread is baked, carefully remove it from the machine and let it cool on a wire rack before slicing.

Nutritional Info: Calories: 220 | Fat: 4g | Carbs: 40g | Protein: 6g

Bread Machine Function: Sweet Bread Setting

Cinnamon Swirl Bread

Prep: 15 mins | Cook: 3 hours | Serves: 1 loaf

Ingredients:
- **US:** 1 cup warm milk, 2 tablespoons butter (softened), 1 egg, 3 cups bread flour, 1/4 cup white sugar, 1 1/2 teaspoons salt, 2 teaspoons bread machine yeast, 2 tablespoons ground cinnamon, 1/4 cup brown sugar
- **UK:** 240ml warm milk, 30g butter (softened), 1 egg, 360g bread flour, 50g white sugar, 1 1/2 teaspoons salt, 7g bread machine yeast, 30g ground cinnamon, 50g brown sugar

Instructions:
1. Add warm milk, softened butter, egg, bread flour, white sugar, salt, and yeast to the bread machine pan according to the manufacturer's instructions.
2. Select the Basic or White Bread setting and start the machine. Allow it to knead the dough and complete the first rise cycle.
3. When the machine beeps to signal adding extras, such as cinnamon swirl ingredients, sprinkle ground cinnamon and brown sugar evenly over the dough.
4. Continue the machine's cycle until it completes the final rise and bake.
5. Once baked, remove the cinnamon swirl bread from the bread machine and let it cool on a wire rack before slicing.

Nutritional Info: Calories: 210 | Fat: 4g | Carbs: 38g | Protein: 6g

Bread Machine Function: Basic or White Bread Setting

Luscious Lemon Bread

Prep: 10 mins | Cook: 3 hours | Serves: 1 loaf

Ingredients:
- **US:** 1 cup warm water, 2 tablespoons vegetable oil, 1 lemon (zest and juice), 3 cups bread flour, 1/4 cup white sugar, 1 1/2 teaspoons salt, 2 teaspoons bread machine yeast
- **UK:** 240ml warm water, 30g vegetable oil, 1 lemon (zest and juice), 360g bread flour, 50g white sugar, 1 1/2 teaspoons salt, 7g bread machine yeast

Instructions:
1. Place warm water, vegetable oil, lemon zest, lemon juice, bread flour, white sugar, salt, and yeast in the bread machine pan.
2. Select the Basic or White Bread setting and start the machine. Allow it to knead the dough and complete the first rise cycle.
3. Once the dough is ready, let the machine complete the final rise and bake.
4. When done, remove the lemon bread from the machine and transfer it to a wire rack to cool completely before slicing.

Nutritional Info: Calories: 180 | Fat: 3g | Carbs: 34g | Protein: 5g

Bread Machine Function: Basic or White Bread Setting

Orange Zest Bread

Prep: 10 mins | Cook: 3 hours | Serves: 1 loaf

Ingredients:
- **US:** 1 cup orange juice, 2 tablespoons unsalted butter (softened), 1 tablespoon orange zest, 3 cups bread flour, 1/4 cup granulated sugar, 1 1/2 teaspoons salt, 2 teaspoons bread machine yeast

- **UK:** 240ml orange juice, 30g unsalted butter (softened), 1 tablespoon orange zest, 360g bread flour, 50g granulated sugar, 1 1/2 teaspoons salt, 7g bread machine yeast

Instructions:
1. Pour the orange juice into the bread machine pan, then add the softened butter and orange zest.
2. Add the bread flour, granulated sugar, salt, and yeast on top of the wet ingredients in the pan.
3. Select the Basic or White Bread setting on your bread machine and start the cycle.
4. Allow the machine to knead the dough and complete the first rise.
5. Once the first rise is finished, let the machine continue with the final rise and bake.
6. When the bread is done, carefully remove it from the machine and place it on a wire rack to cool before slicing.

Nutritional Info: Calories: 190 | Fat: 3g | Carbs: 36g | Protein: 5g

Bread Machine Function: Basic or White Bread Setting

Banana Bliss Bread

Prep: 15 mins | Cook: 3 hours | Serves: 1 loaf

Ingredients:
- **US:** 3 ripe bananas (mashed), 2 tablespoons honey, 2 tablespoons vegetable oil, 1 egg, 3 cups bread flour, 1/4 cup granulated sugar, 1 1/2 teaspoons salt, 2 teaspoons bread machine yeast
- **UK:** 3 ripe bananas (mashed), 30ml honey, 30ml vegetable oil, 1 egg, 360g bread flour, 50g granulated sugar, 1 1/2 teaspoons salt, 7g bread machine yeast

Instructions:
1. In the bread machine pan, combine the mashed bananas, honey, vegetable oil, and egg.
2. Add the bread flour, granulated sugar, salt, and yeast on top of the wet ingredients in the pan.
3. Select the Basic or White Bread setting on your bread machine and start the cycle.
4. Allow the machine to knead the dough and complete the first rise.
5. Once the first rise is finished, let the machine continue with the final rise and bake.
6. After baking, remove the banana bread from the machine and let it cool on a wire rack before slicing.

Nutritional Info: Calories: 200 | Fat: 4g | Carbs: 38g | Protein: 5g

Bread Machine Function: Basic or White Bread Setting

Zucchini Harvest Bread

Prep: 15 mins | Cook: 3 hours | Serves: 1 loaf

Ingredients:
- **US:** 1 cup shredded zucchini, 1/2 cup chopped walnuts, 3 cups bread flour, 1/4 cup granulated sugar, 1 1/2 teaspoons salt, 2 teaspoons bread machine yeast
- **UK:** 240ml shredded zucchini, 70g chopped walnuts, 360g bread flour, 50g granulated sugar, 1 1/2 teaspoons salt, 7g bread machine yeast

Instructions:
1. Prepare the shredded zucchini and chop the walnuts, then add them to the bread machine pan.
2. Add the bread flour, granulated sugar, salt, and yeast on top of the zucchini and walnuts in the pan.
3. Select the Basic or White Bread setting on your bread machine and start the cycle.
4. Allow the machine to knead the dough and complete the first rise.

5. Once the first rise is finished, let the machine continue with the final rise and bake.
6. Remove the zucchini bread from the machine when done and let it cool before slicing.

Nutritional Info: Calories: 210 | Fat: 5g | Carbs: 38g | Protein: 6g

Bread Machine Function: Basic or White Bread Setting

Autumn Pumpkin Bread

Prep: 15 mins | Cook: 3 hours | Serves: 1 loaf

Ingredients:
- **US:** 1 cup canned pumpkin puree, 1 teaspoon ground cinnamon, 1/2 teaspoon ground nutmeg, 3 cups bread flour, 1/4 cup granulated sugar, 1 1/2 teaspoons salt, 2 teaspoons bread machine yeast
- **UK:** 240ml canned pumpkin puree, 1 teaspoon ground cinnamon, 1/2 teaspoon ground nutmeg, 360g bread flour, 50g granulated sugar, 1 1/2 teaspoons salt, 7g bread machine yeast

Instructions:
1. Combine the canned pumpkin puree, ground cinnamon, and ground nutmeg in a bowl.
2. Pour the pumpkin mixture into the bread machine pan.
3. Add the bread flour, granulated sugar, salt, and yeast on top of the pumpkin mixture in the pan.
4. Select the Basic or White Bread setting on your bread machine and start the cycle.
5. Allow the machine to knead the dough and complete the first rise.
6. Once the first rise is finished, let the machine continue with the final rise and bake.
7. Remove the pumpkin bread from the machine when done and let it cool before slicing.

Nutritional Info: Calories: 200 | Fat: 1g | Carbs: 42g | Protein: 6g

Bread Machine Function: Basic or White Bread Setting

Cranberry Orange Bread

Prep: 15 mins | Cook: 3 hours | Serves: 1 loaf

Ingredients:
- **US:** 1/2 cup dried cranberries, 2 tablespoons orange zest, 3 cups bread flour, 1/4 cup granulated sugar, 1 1/2 teaspoons salt, 2 teaspoons bread machine yeast
- **UK:** 70g dried cranberries, 30ml orange zest, 360g bread flour, 50g granulated sugar, 1 1/2 teaspoons salt, 7g bread machine yeast

Instructions:
1. Mix the dried cranberries and orange zest in a bowl.
2. Add the cranberry and orange mixture to the bread machine pan.
3. Add the bread flour, granulated sugar, salt, and yeast on top of the cranberry mixture in the pan.
4. Select the Basic or White Bread setting on your bread machine and start the cycle.
5. Allow the machine to knead the dough and complete the first rise.
6. Once the first rise is finished, let the machine continue with the final rise and bake.
7. Remove the cranberry orange bread from the machine when done and let it cool before slicing.

Nutritional Info: Calories: 210 | Fat: 1g | Carbs: 45g | Protein: 6g

Bread Machine Function: Basic or White Bread Setting

Chocolate Chip Banana Bread

Prep: 15 mins | Cook: 3 hours | Serves: 1 loaf

Ingredients:
- **US:** 2 ripe bananas (mashed), 1/2 cup chocolate chips, 3 cups bread flour, 1/4 cup granulated sugar, 1 1/2 teaspoons salt, 2 teaspoons bread machine yeast
- **UK:** 2 ripe bananas (mashed), 70g chocolate chips, 360g bread flour, 50g granulated sugar, 1 1/2 teaspoons salt, 7g bread machine yeast

Instructions:
1. Mash the ripe bananas in a bowl.
2. Stir in the chocolate chips with the mashed bananas.
3. Transfer the banana and chocolate mixture to the bread machine pan.
4. Add the bread flour, granulated sugar, salt, and yeast on top of the banana mixture in the pan.
5. Select the Basic or White Bread setting on your bread machine and start the cycle.
6. Allow the machine to knead the dough and complete the first rise.
7. Once the first rise is finished, let the machine continue with the final rise and bake.
8. Remove the chocolate chip banana bread from the machine when done and let it cool before slicing.

Nutritional Info: Calories: 220 | Fat: 2g | Carbs: 47g | Protein: 6g

Bread Machine Function: Basic or White Bread Setting

CHAPTER FOUR: FLATBREADS AND PIZZAS

Perfect Pizza Dough

Prep: 10 mins | Cook: 2 hours | Serves: 2 large pizzas

Ingredients:
- **US:** 1 cup warm water, 2 1/4 teaspoons active dry yeast, 2 1/2 cups bread flour, 2 tablespoons olive oil, 1 teaspoon sugar, 1 teaspoon salt
- **UK:** 240ml warm water, 7g active dry yeast, 300g bread flour, 30ml olive oil, 5g sugar, 5g salt

Instructions:
1. Add warm water, yeast, and sugar to the bread machine pan. Let it sit for 5 minutes until frothy.
2. Add bread flour, olive oil, and salt to the pan.
3. Select the Pizza Dough setting on your bread machine and start the cycle.
4. Once the dough is ready, remove it from the machine and divide it into two equal portions.
5. Roll out each portion into a pizza crust of your desired thickness.
6. Add your favorite pizza toppings and bake in a preheated oven at 425°F (220°C) for 1215 minutes or until the crust is golden brown.

Nutritional Info: Calories: 120 | Fat: 3g | Carbs: 20g | Protein: 4g

Bread Machine Function: Pizza Dough Setting

Herb Focaccia

Prep: 15 mins | Cook: 2 hours | Serves: 1 loaf

Ingredients:
- **US:** 1 cup warm water, 2 1/4 teaspoons active dry yeast, 2 1/2 cups bread flour, 2 tablespoons olive oil, 1 tablespoon dried herbs (rosemary, thyme, oregano), 1 teaspoon salt
- **UK:** 240ml warm water, 7g active dry yeast, 300g bread flour, 30ml olive oil, 15g dried herbs (rosemary, thyme, oregano), 5g salt

Instructions:
1. Place warm water and yeast in the bread machine pan. Let it sit for 5 minutes.
2. Add bread flour, olive oil, dried herbs, and salt to the pan.
3. Select the Dough setting on your bread machine and start the cycle.
4. Once the dough is ready, remove it from the machine and shape it into a rectangle on a baking sheet.
5. Cover and let it rise for 3045 minutes.
6. Preheat the oven to 400°F (200°C).
7. Use your fingers to create dimples on the dough surface. Drizzle with olive oil and sprinkle with additional herbs and salt.
8. Bake for 2025 minutes or until golden brown.

Nutritional Info: Calories: 150 | Fat: 4g | Carbs: 24g | Protein: 5g

Bread Machine Function: Dough Setting

Garlic Naan

Prep: 15 mins | Cook: 1 hour | Serves: 4 naans

Ingredients:
- **US:** 1 cup warm water, 2 1/4 teaspoons active dry yeast, 3 cups allpurpose flour, 2 tablespoons plain yogurt, 2 tablespoons melted butter, 2 cloves garlic (minced), 1 teaspoon sugar, 1/2 teaspoon salt, additional melted butter for brushing
- **UK:** 240ml warm water, 7g active dry yeast, 360g allpurpose flour, 30ml plain yogurt, 30ml melted butter, 2 cloves garlic (minced), 5g sugar, 3g salt, additional melted butter for brushing

Instructions:
1. Add warm water, yeast, and sugar to the bread machine pan. Let it sit for 5 minutes.
2. Add allpurpose flour, plain yogurt, melted butter, minced garlic, and salt to the pan.
3. Select the Dough setting on your bread machine and start the cycle.
4. Once the dough is ready, divide it into 4 equal portions and shape each into a ball.
5. On a floured surface, roll out each ball into an oval or round shape, about 1/4 inch thick.
6. Heat a skillet or griddle over mediumhigh heat.
7. Cook each naan for 23 minutes on each side, or until golden brown and cooked through.
8. Brush each naan with melted butter before serving.

Nutritional Info: Calories: 280 | Fat: 7g | Carbs: 45g | Protein: 8g

Bread Machine Function: Dough Setting

Pita Bread

Prep: 15 mins | Cook: 10 mins | Serves: 8 pitas

Ingredients:
- **US:** 1 cup warm water, 2 1/4 teaspoons active dry yeast, 3 cups allpurpose flour, 1 teaspoon salt, 1 tablespoon olive oil
- **UK:** 240ml warm water, 7g active dry yeast, 360g allpurpose flour, 5g salt, 15ml olive oil

Instructions:
1. Add warm water and yeast to the bread machine pan. Let it sit for 5 minutes.
2. Add allpurpose flour, salt, and olive oil to the pan.
3. Select the Dough setting on your bread machine and start the cycle.
4. Once the dough is ready, divide it into 8 equal portions and shape each into a ball.
5. On a floured surface, roll out each ball into a circle, about 1/4 inch thick.
6. Preheat a skillet or griddle over mediumhigh heat.
7. Cook each pita for 23 minutes on each side, or until puffed up and lightly browned.
8. Serve warm or store in an airtight container once cooled.

Nutritional Info: Calories: 150 | Fat: 2g | Carbs: 28g | Protein: 5g

Bread Machine Function: Dough Setting

Tortillas

Prep: 15 mins | Cook: 20 mins | Serves: 12 tortillas

Ingredients:
- **US:** 2 cups allpurpose flour, 1/2 teaspoon salt, 3/4 cup warm water, 3 tablespoons vegetable oil
- **UK:** 250g plain flour, 3g salt, 180ml warm water, 45ml vegetable oil

Instructions:
1. In the bread machine pan, combine flour, salt, warm water, and vegetable oil.
2. Select the Dough setting and start the cycle.
3. Once the dough is ready, divide it into 12 equal portions and shape each into a ball.
4. On a floured surface, roll out each ball into a thin circle.
5. Heat a skillet or griddle over mediumhigh heat.
6. Cook each tortilla for about 30 seconds on each side, or until lightly browned and bubbly.
7. Repeat with the remaining dough balls.
8. Serve warm or store in an airtight container.

Nutritional Info: Calories: 110 | Fat: 3g | Carbs: 18g | Protein: 2g

Bread Machine Function: Dough Setting

Chapati

Prep: 10 mins | Cook: 15 mins | Serves: 8 chapatis

Ingredients:
- **US:** 2 cups whole wheat flour, 1/2 teaspoon salt, 3/4 cup warm water
- **UK:** 250g wholemeal flour, 3g salt, 180ml warm water

Instructions:
1. Combine whole wheat flour, salt, and warm water in the bread machine pan.
2. Select the Dough setting and start the cycle.
3. Once the dough is ready, divide it into 8 equal portions and shape each into a ball.
4. On a floured surface, roll out each ball into a thin circle.
5. Heat a skillet or griddle over mediumhigh heat.
6. Cook each chapati for about 1 minute on each side, or until lightly browned and cooked through.
7. Stack cooked chapatis on a plate and cover with a clean kitchen towel to keep warm.

Nutritional Info: Calories: 100 | Fat: 1g | Carbs: 20g | Protein: 3g

Bread Machine Function: Dough Setting

Calzone Dough

Prep: 15 mins | Cook: 20 mins | Serves: 4 calzones

Ingredients:
- **US:** 2 cups bread flour, 1 teaspoon salt, 1 tablespoon sugar, 1 tablespoon olive oil, 3/4 cup warm water, 2 1/4 teaspoons active dry yeast
- **UK:** 250g strong white bread flour, 5g salt, 12g sugar, 15ml olive oil, 180ml warm water, 7g active dry yeast

Instructions:
1. Add warm water, olive oil, salt, sugar, bread flour, and active dry yeast to the bread machine pan in the order recommended by the manufacturer.
2. Select the Dough setting and start the cycle.
3. Once the dough is ready, divide it into 4 equal portions and shape each into a ball.
4. On a floured surface, roll out each ball into a thin circle or oval shape.
5. Fill half of each dough circle with desired calzone fillings, leaving a border around the edges.
6. Fold the other half of the dough over the filling and press the edges to seal.
7. Transfer the calzones to a baking sheet lined with parchment paper.
8. Bake in a preheated oven at 400°F (200°C) for 1520 minutes, or until the crust is golden brown.

Nutritional Info: Calories: 300 | Fat: 5g | Carbs: 55g | Protein: 8g

Bread Machine Function: Dough Setting

Stromboli

Prep: 20 mins | Cook: 25 mins | Serves: 4 servings

Ingredients:
- **US:** 2 cups bread flour, 1 teaspoon salt, 1 tablespoon sugar, 1 tablespoon olive oil, 3/4 cup warm water, 2 1/4 teaspoons active dry yeast, 1/2 cup marinara sauce, 1 cup shredded mozzarella cheese, 1/4 cup sliced pepperoni, 1/4 cup sliced black olives, 1/4 cup sliced bell peppers
- **UK:** 250g strong white bread flour, 5g salt, 12g sugar, 15ml olive oil, 180ml warm water, 7g active dry yeast, 120ml marinara sauce, 100g shredded mozzarella cheese, 25g sliced pepperoni, 25g sliced black olives, 25g sliced bell peppers

Instructions:
1. Place warm water, olive oil, salt, sugar, bread flour, and active dry yeast into the bread machine pan according to the manufacturer's instructions.
2. Select the Dough setting and start the cycle.
3. Once the dough is ready, roll it out into a large rectangle on a floured surface.
4. Spread marinara sauce evenly over the dough, leaving a border around the edges.
5. Sprinkle shredded mozzarella cheese over the marinara sauce, then add pepperoni, black olives, and bell peppers.
6. Roll up the dough tightly from one of the long sides, sealing the edge.
7. Place the stromboli seam side down on a baking sheet lined with parchment paper.
8. Bake in a preheated oven at 375°F (190°C) for 25-30 minutes, or until the crust is golden brown and the filling is heated through.

Nutritional Info: Calories: 350 | Fat: 10g | Carbs: 45g | Protein: 15g

Bread Machine Function: Dough Setting

Bagels

Prep: 20 mins | Cook: 25 mins | Serves: 8 bagels

Ingredients:
- **US:** 1 1/2 cups warm water, 2 tablespoons white sugar, 1 1/2 teaspoons salt, 3 1/2 cups bread flour, 2 1/4 teaspoons active dry yeast, 1 tablespoon cornmeal (for dusting)
- **UK:** 350ml warm water, 25g white sugar, 10g salt, 430g strong white bread flour, 7g active dry yeast, 15g cornmeal (for dusting)

Instructions:
1. Add warm water, sugar, salt, bread flour, and active dry yeast to the bread machine pan in the order recommended by the manufacturer.
2. Select the Dough setting and start the cycle.
3. Once the dough is ready, divide it into 8 equal portions and shape each portion into a ball.
4. Poke a hole in the center of each ball with your finger and gently stretch the dough to form a ring.
5. Place the shaped bagels on a baking sheet sprinkled with cornmeal.
6. Cover the bagels with a clean kitchen towel and let them rise for about 20 minutes.
7. Preheat the oven to 375°F (190°C).
8. Bring a large pot of water to a boil and carefully drop the bagels into the boiling water, boiling them for 12 minutes on each side.
9. Remove the boiled bagels from the water and place them back on the baking sheet.
10. Bake the bagels in the preheated oven for 2025 minutes, or until they are golden brown.

Nutritional Info: Calories: 210 | Fat: 0.5g | Carbs: 42g | Protein: 6g

Bread Machine Function: Dough Setting

English Muffins

Prep: 20 mins | Cook: 15 mins | Serves: 12 muffins

Ingredients:
- **US:** 1 cup milk, 2 tablespoons white sugar, 1 teaspoon salt, 1 tablespoon butter, 1 egg, 3 cups bread flour, 1 1/2 teaspoons active dry yeast, cornmeal (for dusting)
- **UK:** 240ml milk, 25g white sugar, 5g salt, 15g butter, 1 egg, 380g strong white bread flour, 7g active dry yeast, cornmeal (for dusting)

Instructions:
1. Warm the milk in a microwavesafe bowl until it reaches about 110°F (45°C).
2. In the bread machine pan, combine warm milk, sugar, salt, melted butter, beaten egg, bread flour, and active dry yeast.
3. Select the Dough setting and start the cycle.
4. Once the dough is ready, turn it out onto a lightly floured surface and roll it out to about 1/2 inch (1.25 cm) thickness.
5. Use a round cookie cutter or the rim of a glass to cut out circles of dough.
6. Sprinkle a baking sheet with cornmeal and place the dough circles on it, spacing them apart.
7. Cover the dough circles with a clean kitchen towel and let them rise for about 30 minutes.
8. Heat a lightly greased griddle or skillet over medium heat.
9. Cook the English muffins on the griddle for about 57 minutes on each side, or until they are golden brown and cooked through.
10. Allow the English muffins to cool before slicing and toasting.

Nutritional Info: Calories: 120 | Fat: 2g | Carbs: 21g | Protein: 4g

Bread Machine Function: Dough Setting

Pretzels

Prep: 30 mins | Cook: 12 mins | Serves: 12 pretzels

Ingredients:
- **US:** 1 1/2 cups warm water, 1 tablespoon white sugar, 1 tablespoon active dry yeast, 4 cups bread flour, 1/2 teaspoon salt, 2 tablespoons baking soda, 2 cups hot water, coarse salt (for topping), 1/4 cup melted butter (optional)
- **UK:** 350ml warm water, 12g white sugar, 7g active dry yeast, 500g strong white bread flour, 2.5g salt, 30g baking soda, 475ml hot water, coarse salt (for topping), 60g melted butter (optional)

Instructions:
1. In the bread machine pan, combine warm water, sugar, and active dry yeast. Let it sit for about 5 minutes until foamy.
2. Add bread flour and salt to the yeast mixture.
3. Select the Dough setting and start the cycle.
4. Once the dough is ready, preheat the oven to 450°F (230°C) and line a baking sheet with parchment paper.
5. Divide the dough into 12 equal portions and roll each portion into a rope.
6. Shape each rope into a pretzel by forming a U shape, then crossing the ends over each other and pressing them down onto the bottom of the U.
7. In a shallow dish, dissolve baking soda in hot water.
8. Dip each pretzel into the baking soda solution, then place them on the prepared baking sheet.
9. Sprinkle coarse salt over the pretzels.
10. Bake the pretzels in the preheated oven for 1012 minutes, or until they are golden brown.
11. Optional: Brush the baked pretzels with melted butter for added flavor.

Nutritional Info: Calories: 180 | Fat: 2g | Carbs: 35g | Protein: 6g

Bread Machine Function: Dough Setting

Breadsticks

Prep: 20 mins | Cook: 15 mins | Serves: 12 breadsticks

Ingredients:
- **US:** 1 cup warm water, 2 tablespoons olive oil, 1 tablespoon white sugar, 1 teaspoon salt, 3 cups bread flour, 2 1/4 teaspoons active dry yeast, 2 tablespoons grated Parmesan cheese, 1 teaspoon garlic powder, 1 teaspoon dried basil, 1 teaspoon dried oregano, 2 tablespoons butter (melted), 1/4 cup grated Parmesan cheese (for topping)
- **UK:** 240ml warm water, 30ml olive oil, 12g white sugar, 5g salt, 380g strong white bread flour, 7g active dry yeast, 30g grated Parmesan cheese, 5g garlic powder, 5g dried basil, 5g dried oregano, 30g butter (melted), 30g grated Parmesan cheese (for topping)

Instructions:
1. Add warm water, olive oil, sugar, salt, bread flour, and active dry yeast to the bread machine pan in the order recommended by the manufacturer.
2. Select the Dough setting and start the cycle.
3. Once the dough is ready, preheat the oven to 375°F (190°C) and line a baking sheet with parchment paper.
4. Turn the dough out onto a lightly floured surface and divide it into 12 equal portions.
5. Roll each portion into a breadstick shape and place them on the prepared baking sheet.
6. In a small bowl, mix together grated Parmesan cheese, garlic powder, dried basil, and dried oregano.
7. Brush the breadsticks with melted butter and sprinkle the Parmesan cheese mixture over the top.
8. Bake the breadsticks in the preheated oven for 1215 minutes, or until they are golden brown.

Nutritional Info: Calories: 160 | Fat: 5g | Carbs: 23g | Protein: 5g

Bread Machine Function: Dough Setting

Crackers

Prep: 15 mins | Cook: 12 mins | Serves: 24 crackers

Ingredients:
- **US:** 1 cup allpurpose flour, 1/2 teaspoon salt, 1/2 teaspoon baking powder, 1/4 cup cold unsalted butter (cut into small cubes), 1/4 cup cold water, 1 tablespoon sesame seeds (optional), 1 tablespoon poppy seeds (optional), 1 tablespoon dried herbs (such as rosemary or thyme, optional), coarse salt for sprinkling
- **UK:** 125g plain flour, 2.5g salt, 2.5g baking powder, 55g cold unsalted butter (cut into small cubes), 60ml cold water, 15g sesame seeds (optional), 15g poppy seeds (optional), 15g dried herbs (such as rosemary or thyme, optional), coarse salt for sprinkling

Instructions:
1. In the bread machine pan, combine the flour, salt, and baking powder.
2. Add the cold butter cubes and pulse the machine until the mixture resembles coarse crumbs.
3. Slowly add the cold water while pulsing the machine until the dough comes together.
4. Remove the dough from the bread machine and wrap it in plastic wrap. Chill in the refrigerator for at least 30 minutes.
5. Preheat the oven to 375°F (190°C) and line a baking sheet with parchment paper.
6. On a lightly floured surface, roll out the dough thinly.
7. Use a cookie cutter or knife to cut the dough into desired shapes.
8. Place the crackers on the prepared baking sheet. If desired, sprinkle sesame seeds, poppy seeds, dried herbs, or coarse salt on top.
9. Bake for 1012 minutes, or until the crackers are golden brown and crisp.

Nutritional Info: Calories: 45 | Fat: 2g | Carbs: 5g | Protein: 1g

Bread Machine Function: Pulse or Manual Mode

Lavash

Prep: 20 mins | Cook: 15 mins | Serves: 12 lavash

Ingredients:

   US: 1 cup allpurpose flour, 1/2 teaspoon salt, 1 tablespoon olive oil, 1/3 cup water, sesame seeds (optional), poppy seeds (optional), dried herbs (such as thyme or oregano, optional)

   UK: 125g plain flour, 2.5g salt, 15ml olive oil, 80ml water, sesame seeds (optional), poppy seeds (optional), dried herbs (such as thyme or oregano, optional)

Instructions:
1. In the bread machine pan, combine the flour and salt.
2. Add the olive oil and water to the dry ingredients.
3. Select the Dough setting and start the cycle.
4. Once the dough is ready, preheat the oven to 400°F (200°C) and line a baking sheet with parchment paper.
5. Divide the dough into 12 equal portions and roll each portion into a thin rectangle on a lightly floured surface.
6. Place the rolledout lavash onto the prepared baking sheet.
7. If desired, sprinkle sesame seeds, poppy seeds, or dried herbs over the lavash.
8. Bake for 1215 minutes, or until the lavash is golden brown and crisp.

Nutritional Info: Calories: 60 | Fat: 2g | Carbs: 10g | Protein: 2g

Bread Machine Function: Dough Setting

Pita Chips

Prep: 10 mins | Cook: 10 mins | Serves: 4 servings

Ingredients:
- **US:** 4 whole wheat pita bread rounds, 2 tablespoons olive oil, 1 teaspoon garlic powder, 1 teaspoon dried oregano, salt to taste
- **UK:** 4 whole wheat pita bread rounds, 30ml olive oil, 2.5g garlic powder, 2.5g dried oregano, salt to taste

Instructions:
1. Preheat the bread machine to the Baking mode at 375°F (190°C).
2. Cut each pita bread round into 8 wedges.
3. In a small bowl, mix together the olive oil, garlic powder, and dried oregano.
4. Brush the pita wedges with the olive oil mixture on both sides.
5. Place the pita wedges in a single layer on the baking tray of the bread machine.
6. Sprinkle salt over the pita chips.
7. Bake in the preheated bread machine for about 810 minutes, or until the chips are golden brown and crispy.
8. Remove from the bread machine and let them cool slightly before serving.

Nutritional Info: Calories: 160 | Fat: 8g | Carbs: 20g | Protein: 4g

Bread Machine Function: Baking Mode

Tortilla Chips

Prep: 10 mins | Cook: 10 mins | Serves: 4 servings

Ingredients:
- **US:** 4 large flour tortillas, 2 tablespoons olive oil, 1 teaspoon chili powder, 1/2 teaspoon garlic powder, salt to taste
- **UK:** 4 large flour tortillas, 30ml olive oil, 2.5g chili powder, 2.5g garlic powder, salt to taste

Instructions:
1. Preheat the bread machine to the Baking mode at 375°F (190°C).
2. Stack the tortillas on top of each other and cut them into wedges.
3. In a small bowl, mix together the olive oil, chili powder, and garlic powder.
4. Brush both sides of the tortilla wedges with the olive oil mixture.
5. Place the tortilla wedges in a single layer on the baking tray of the bread machine.
6. Sprinkle salt over the tortilla chips.
7. Bake in the preheated bread machine for about 810 minutes, or until the chips are golden brown and crispy.
8. Remove from the bread machine and let them cool slightly before serving.

Nutritional Info: Calories: 150 | Fat: 8g | Carbs: 16g | Protein: 2g

Bread Machine Function: Baking Mode

Herb Bread

Prep: 15 mins | Cook: 3 hours | Serves: 1 loaf

Ingredients:
- **US:** 1 cup water, 2 tablespoons olive oil, 3 cups bread flour, 2 tablespoons sugar, 1 teaspoon salt, 2 teaspoons dried mixed herbs (such as rosemary, thyme, and oregano), 2 teaspoons active dry yeast
- **UK:** 240ml water, 30ml olive oil, 375g strong white bread flour, 30g sugar, 5g salt, 5g dried mixed herbs (such as rosemary, thyme, and oregano), 7g active dry yeast

Instructions:
1. Add the water, olive oil, bread flour, sugar, salt, dried herbs, and yeast to the bread machine pan in the order recommended by the manufacturer.
2. Select the Basic or White Bread setting on the bread machine and start the cycle.
3. Once the baking cycle is complete, remove the bread from the machine and let it cool on a wire rack before slicing.

Nutritional Info: Calories: 120 | Fat: 3g | Carbs: 20g | Protein: 3g

Bread Machine Function: Basic or White Bread Setting

Garlic Knots

Prep: 15 mins | Cook: 25 mins | Serves: 8 servings

Ingredients:
- **US:** 1 cup warm water (110°F/45°C), 1 tablespoon sugar, 2 1/4 teaspoons active dry yeast, 2 tablespoons olive oil, 3 cups allpurpose flour, 1 teaspoon salt, 4 cloves garlic (minced), 2 tablespoons unsalted butter (melted), 2 tablespoons chopped fresh parsley

- **UK:** 240ml warm water (110°F/45°C), 15g sugar, 7g active dry yeast, 30ml olive oil, 375g plain flour, 5g salt, 4 cloves garlic (minced), 30g unsalted butter (melted), 2 tablespoons chopped fresh parsley

Instructions:
1. In the bread machine pan, combine warm water, sugar, and yeast. Let it sit for 510 minutes until foamy.
2. Add olive oil, flour, and salt to the pan. Select the Dough setting and start the cycle.
3. Once the dough cycle is complete, transfer the dough to a lightly floured surface and knead it a few times.
4. Preheat the bread machine to 375°F (190°C) on the Bake setting.
5. Divide the dough into 8 equal pieces and roll each piece into a rope about 6 inches long.
6. Tie each rope into a knot and place them on a baking sheet lined with parchment paper.
7. In a small bowl, mix together minced garlic and melted butter. Brush the garlic butter mixture over the knots.
8. Bake in the preheated bread machine for 2025 minutes, or until the knots are golden brown.
9. Remove from the bread machine and sprinkle with chopped parsley before serving.

Nutritional Info: Calories: 210 | Fat: 6g | Carbs: 33g | Protein: 5g

Bread Machine Function: Dough Setting, Bake Setting

CHAPTER FIVE: GLUTENFREE AND SPECIALTY BREADS

GlutenFree Bread

Prep: 15 mins | Cook: 3 hours | Serves: 1 loaf

Ingredients:
- **US:** 1 cup warm water (110°F/45°C), 2 tablespoons honey, 2 1/4 teaspoons active dry yeast, 3 cups glutenfree allpurpose flour, 1 teaspoon salt, 2 tablespoons olive oil
- **UK:** 240ml warm water (110°F/45°C), 30g honey, 7g active dry yeast, 375g glutenfree allpurpose flour, 5g salt, 30ml olive oil

Instructions:
1. Add warm water, honey, and yeast to the bread machine pan. Allow it to sit for 510 minutes until foamy.
2. Add the glutenfree flour, salt, and olive oil to the pan.
3. Select the GlutenFree setting on your bread machine and start the cycle.
4. Once the cycle is complete, remove the bread from the machine and let it cool before slicing.

Nutritional Info: Calories: 150 | Fat: 4g | Carbs: 28g | Protein: 2g

Bread Machine Function: GlutenFree Setting

Keto Bread

Prep: 10 mins | Cook: 3 hours | Serves: 1 loaf

Ingredients:
- **US:** 6 large eggs, 1/2 cup coconut flour, 1/4 cup melted butter, 1 teaspoon baking powder, 1/2 teaspoon salt
- **UK:** 6 large eggs, 60g coconut flour, 60g melted butter, 5g baking powder, 3g salt

Instructions:
1. Crack the eggs into the bread machine pan.
2. Add melted butter, coconut flour, baking powder, and salt to the pan.
3. Select the Quick Bread setting on your bread machine and start the cycle.
4. Once done, remove the bread from the machine and allow it to cool before slicing.

Nutritional Info: Calories: 140 | Fat: 10g | Carbs: 5g | Protein: 6g

Bread Machine Function: Quick Bread Setting

Paleo Bread

Prep: 10 mins | Cook: 3 hours | Serves: 1 loaf

Ingredients:
- **US:** 4 large eggs, 1/2 cup almond flour, 1/4 cup coconut flour, 1/4 cup melted coconut oil, 1 teaspoon baking powder, 1/2 teaspoon salt
- **UK:** 4 large eggs, 60g almond flour, 60g coconut flour, 60ml melted coconut oil, 5g baking powder, 3g salt

Instructions:
1. Crack the eggs into the bread machine pan.
2. Add almond flour, coconut flour, melted coconut oil, baking powder, and salt to the pan.
3. Select the GlutenFree setting on your bread machine and start the cycle.
4. Once the cycle is complete, let the bread cool in the pan for a few minutes before transferring it to a wire rack.

Nutritional Info: Calories: 160 | Fat: 12g | Carbs: 5g | Protein: 7g

Bread Machine Function: GlutenFree Setting

Vegan Bread

Prep: 10 mins | Cook: 3 hours | Serves: 1 loaf

Ingredients:
- **US:** 1 cup warm almond milk, 2 tablespoons maple syrup, 2 1/4 teaspoons active dry yeast, 3 cups allpurpose flour, 1 teaspoon salt, 2 tablespoons olive oil
- **UK:** 240ml warm almond milk, 30ml maple syrup, 7g active dry yeast, 375g allpurpose flour, 5g salt, 30ml olive oil

Instructions:
1. Pour warm almond milk and maple syrup into the bread machine pan.
2. Sprinkle yeast over the liquid mixture and let it sit for 510 minutes until foamy.
3. Add allpurpose flour, salt, and olive oil to the pan.
4. Select the Basic or White Bread setting on your bread machine and start the cycle.
5. Once baked, remove the bread from the machine and allow it to cool before slicing.

Nutritional Info: Calories: 180 | Fat: 4g | Carbs: 32g | Protein: 4g

Bread Machine Function: Basic or White Bread Setting

NutFree Bread

Prep: 15 mins | Cook: 3 hours | Serves: 1 loaf

Ingredients:
- **US:** 1 1/2 cups oat flour, 1/2 cup tapioca flour, 1/4 cup coconut flour, 1 teaspoon baking powder, 1/2 teaspoon salt, 1 cup warm water, 2 tablespoons olive oil
- **UK:** 180g oat flour, 60g tapioca flour, 30g coconut flour, 5g baking powder, 3g salt, 240ml warm water, 30ml olive oil

Instructions:
1. Combine oat flour, tapioca flour, coconut flour, baking powder, and salt in a bowl.
2. Pour warm water and olive oil into the bread machine pan.
3. Add the dry ingredients to the pan.
4. Select the GlutenFree setting on your bread machine and start the cycle.
5. Once baked, let the bread cool before slicing.

Nutritional Info: Calories: 160 | Fat: 5g | Carbs: 26g | Protein: 3g

Bread Machine Function: GlutenFree Setting

DairyFree Bread

Prep: 10 mins | Cook: 3 hours | Serves: 1 loaf

Ingredients:
- **US:** 1 cup unsweetened almond milk, 2 tablespoons maple syrup, 2 1/4 teaspoons active dry yeast, 3 cups bread flour, 1 teaspoon salt, 2 tablespoons olive oil
- **UK:** 240ml unsweetened almond milk, 30ml maple syrup, 7g active dry yeast, 375g bread flour, 5g salt, 30ml olive oil

Instructions:
1. Warm almond milk and maple syrup in a microwavesafe bowl until it reaches a lukewarm temperature.
2. Pour the almond milk mixture into the bread machine pan.
3. Add active dry yeast to the pan and let it sit for 510 minutes until foamy.
4. Add bread flour, salt, and olive oil to the pan.
5. Select the Basic or White Bread setting on your bread machine and start the cycle.
6. Once the bread is baked, allow it to cool before slicing.

Nutritional Info: Calories: 180 | Fat: 4g | Carbs: 32g | Protein: 4g

Bread Machine Function: Basic or White Bread Setting

LowCarb Bread

Prep: 10 mins | Cook: 3 hours | Serves: 1 loaf

Ingredients:
- **US:** 1 cup almond flour, 1/4 cup coconut flour, 1/4 cup ground flaxseed, 1/4 cup psyllium husk powder, 1 teaspoon baking powder, 1/2 teaspoon salt, 4 large eggs, 1/4 cup olive oil, 1/4 cup unsweetened almond milk

- **UK:** 120g almond flour, 30g coconut flour, 30g ground flaxseed, 30g psyllium husk powder, 5g baking powder, 3g salt, 4 large eggs, 60ml olive oil, 60ml unsweetened almond milk

Instructions:
1. In a large bowl, mix almond flour, coconut flour, ground flaxseed, psyllium husk powder, baking powder, and salt.
2. In a separate bowl, whisk together eggs, olive oil, and almond milk.
3. Pour the wet ingredients into the bread machine pan.
4. Add the dry ingredients to the pan.
5. Select the GlutenFree or LowCarb setting on your bread machine and start the cycle.
6. Once baked, let the bread cool completely before slicing.

Nutritional Info: Calories: 150 | Fat: 10g | Carbs: 8g | Protein: 7g

Bread Machine Function: GlutenFree or LowCarb Setting

HighProtein Bread

Prep: 10 mins | Cook: 3 hours | Serves: 1 loaf

Ingredients:
- **US:** 1 cup whole wheat flour, 1 cup bread flour, 1/2 cup rolled oats, 1/4 cup protein powder, 2 tablespoons honey, 1 teaspoon salt, 1 1/4 cups warm water, 2 tablespoons olive oil, 2 1/4 teaspoons active dry yeast
- **UK:** 120g whole wheat flour, 120g bread flour, 60g rolled oats, 30g protein powder, 30ml honey, 5g salt, 300ml warm water, 30ml olive oil, 7g active dry yeast

Instructions:
1. Combine whole wheat flour, bread flour, rolled oats, protein powder, honey, and salt in a bowl.
2. Pour warm water and olive oil into the bread machine pan.
3. Add the dry ingredients to the pan.
4. Make a small well in the center of the dry ingredients and add the yeast.

5. Select the Whole Wheat or HighProtein setting on your bread machine and start the cycle.
6. Once baked, let the bread cool before slicing.

Nutritional Info: Calories: 160 | Fat: 4g | Carbs: 25g | Protein: 7g

Bread Machine Function: Whole Wheat or HighProtein Setting

Sprouted Grain Bread

Prep: 10 mins | Cook: 3 hours | Serves: 1 loaf

Ingredients:
- **US:** 1 cup sprouted grain flour, 1 1/2 cups bread flour, 1 teaspoon salt, 1 tablespoon honey, 1 tablespoon olive oil, 1 cup warm water, 2 1/4 teaspoons active dry yeast
- **UK:** 120g sprouted grain flour, 180g bread flour, 5g salt, 15ml honey, 15ml olive oil, 240ml warm water, 7g active dry yeast

Instructions:
1. Mix sprouted grain flour, bread flour, and salt in a large bowl.
2. In a separate bowl, combine honey, olive oil, and warm water.
3. Pour the wet ingredients into the bread machine pan.
4. Add the dry ingredients to the pan.
5. Make a small well in the center of the dry ingredients and add the yeast.
6. Select the Whole Wheat or Grain setting on your bread machine and start the cycle.
7. Once baked, let the bread cool before slicing.

Nutritional Info: Calories: 160 | Fat: 3g | Carbs: 30g | Protein: 5g

Bread Machine Function: Whole Wheat or Grain Setting

Quinoa Bread

Prep: 15 mins | Cook: 3 hours | Serves: 1 loaf

Ingredients:
- **US:** 1 cup cooked quinoa, 1 1/2 cups bread flour, 1/2 cup whole wheat flour, 1 teaspoon salt, 2 tablespoons honey, 2 tablespoons olive oil, 1 cup warm water, 2 1/4 teaspoons active dry yeast
- **UK:** 200g cooked quinoa, 180g bread flour, 60g whole wheat flour, 5g salt, 30ml honey, 30ml olive oil, 240ml warm water, 7g active dry yeast

Instructions:
1. In a large bowl, mix cooked quinoa, bread flour, whole wheat flour, and salt.
2. In a separate bowl, combine honey, olive oil, and warm water.
3. Pour the wet ingredients into the bread machine pan.
4. Add the dry ingredients to the pan.
5. Make a small well in the center of the dry ingredients and add the yeast.
6. Select the Whole Wheat or Multigrain setting on your bread machine and start the cycle.
7. Once baked, let the bread cool before slicing.

Nutritional Info: Calories: 170 | Fat: 4g | Carbs: 30g | Protein: 5g

Bread Machine Function: Whole Wheat or Multigrain Setting

Cornbread

Prep: 10 mins | Cook: 2 hours | Serves: 1 loaf

Ingredients:
- **US:** 1 cup cornmeal, 1 cup allpurpose flour, 1 tablespoon baking powder, 1/2 teaspoon salt, 1/4 cup sugar, 1 cup milk, 1/4 cup melted butter, 2 eggs

- **UK:** 120g cornmeal, 120g allpurpose flour, 15ml baking powder, 3g salt, 50g sugar, 240ml milk, 60g melted butter, 2 eggs

Instructions:
1. In a bowl, mix cornmeal, allpurpose flour, baking powder, salt, and sugar.
2. In a separate bowl, whisk together milk, melted butter, and eggs.
3. Pour the wet ingredients into the bread machine pan.
4. Add the dry ingredients to the pan.
5. Select the Quick Bread or Cake setting on your bread machine and start the cycle.
6. Once baked, let the cornbread cool slightly before slicing.

Nutritional Info: Calories: 180 | Fat: 6g | Carbs: 27g | Protein: 4g

Bread Machine Function: Quick Bread or Cake Setting

Biscuits

Prep: 15 mins | Cook: 20 mins | Serves: 12 biscuits

Ingredients:
   US: 2 cups allpurpose flour, 1 tablespoon baking powder, 1 teaspoon salt, 1/2 cup cold butter, 3/4 cup milk

   UK: 250g allpurpose flour, 15ml baking powder, 5g salt, 115g cold butter, 180ml milk

Instructions:
1. In a bowl, sift together allpurpose flour, baking powder, and salt.
2. Cut cold butter into small pieces and mix it into the flour mixture until it resembles coarse crumbs.
3. Stir in milk until a soft dough forms.
4. Turn the dough out onto a floured surface and knead gently a few times.
5. Roll out the dough to 1/2 inch thickness and cut out biscuits using a round cutter.

6. Place the biscuits on a greased baking sheet.
7. Preheat the oven to 425°F (220°C).
8. Bake the biscuits for 1215 minutes or until golden brown.

Nutritional Info: Calories: 160 | Fat: 7g | Carbs: 20g | Protein: 3g

Bread Machine Function: Not applicable, bake in the oven.

Scones

Prep: 15 mins | Cook: 20 mins | Serves: 8 scones

Ingredients:
- **US:** 2 cups allpurpose flour, 1/4 cup sugar, 1 tablespoon baking powder, 1/2 teaspoon salt, 1/3 cup cold butter, 1/2 cup milk, 1 egg, 1 teaspoon vanilla extract
- **UK:** 250g allpurpose flour, 50g sugar, 15ml baking powder, 3g salt, 75g cold butter, 120ml milk, 1 egg, 5ml vanilla extract

Instructions:
1. In a bowl, whisk together allpurpose flour, sugar, baking powder, and salt.
2. Cut cold butter into small pieces and rub it into the flour mixture until it resembles breadcrumbs.
3. In a separate bowl, mix together milk, egg, and vanilla extract.
4. Pour the wet ingredients into the dry ingredients and mix until just combined.
5. Turn the dough out onto a floured surface and gently knead a few times.
6. Pat the dough into a circle about 1 inch thick.
7. Cut the dough into 8 wedges and place them on a greased baking sheet.
8. Preheat the oven to 400°F (200°C).
9. Bake the scones for 1520 minutes or until golden brown.

Nutritional Info: Calories: 220 | Fat: 9g | Carbs: 30g | Protein: 4g

Bread Machine Function: Not applicable, bake in the oven.

Muffins

Prep: 15 mins | Cook: 20 mins | Serves: 12 muffins

Ingredients:
- **US:** 2 cups allpurpose flour, 1/2 cup sugar, 1 tablespoon baking powder, 1/2 teaspoon salt, 1/2 cup milk, 1/2 cup vegetable oil, 2 eggs, 1 teaspoon vanilla extract
- **UK:** 250g allpurpose flour, 100g sugar, 15ml baking powder, 3g salt, 120ml milk, 120ml vegetable oil, 2 eggs, 5ml vanilla extract

Instructions:
1. In a bowl, combine allpurpose flour, sugar, baking powder, and salt.
2. In another bowl, whisk together milk, vegetable oil, eggs, and vanilla extract.
3. Pour the wet ingredients into the dry ingredients and stir until just combined.
4. Line a muffin tin with paper liners or grease with cooking spray.
5. Preheat the oven to 375°F (190°C).
6. Fill each muffin cup about 2/3 full with the batter.
7. Bake the muffins for 1520 minutes or until a toothpick inserted into the center comes out clean.
8. Allow the muffins to cool in the pan for a few minutes before transferring them to a wire rack to cool completely.

Nutritional Info: Calories: 200 | Fat: 8g | Carbs: 28g | Protein: 3g

Bread Machine Function: Not applicable, bake in the oven.

Bagels

Prep: 15 mins | Cook: 20 mins | Serves: 8 bagels

Ingredients:
- **US:** 1 cup warm water, 2 1/4 teaspoons active dry yeast, 2 tablespoons honey, 3 1/2 cups bread flour, 1 1/2 teaspoons salt, 1 tablespoon vegetable oil, 1 egg (for egg wash), toppings of choice (sesame seeds, poppy seeds, etc.)
- **UK:** 240ml warm water, 7g active dry yeast, 30ml honey, 420g bread flour, 7g salt, 15ml vegetable oil, 1 egg (for egg wash), toppings of choice (sesame seeds, poppy seeds, etc.)

1. *Instructions:*
1. In a bowl, combine warm water, active dry yeast, and honey. Let it sit for about 5 minutes until frothy.
2. In a large bowl, mix bread flour and salt.
3. Pour the yeast mixture into the flour mixture and stir until it forms a dough.
4. Knead the dough on a floured surface for about 10 minutes until smooth and elastic.
5. Divide the dough into 8 equal portions and shape each portion into a ball.
6. Flatten each ball slightly and poke a hole in the center with your finger.
7. Stretch the hole slightly to form a bagel shape.
8. Place the shaped bagels on a parchmentlined baking sheet, cover with a clean towel, and let them rise for about 20 minutes.
9. Preheat the oven to 425°F (220°C).
10. Bring a large pot of water to a boil and add the vegetable oil.
11. Boil the bagels, a few at a time, for about 1 minute per side.
12. Remove the bagels from the water and place them back on the baking sheet.
13. Brush the tops of the bagels with egg wash and sprinkle with toppings of your choice.
14. Bake the bagels for 1520 minutes or until golden brown.
15. Allow the bagels to cool before slicing and serving.

Nutritional Info: Calories: 240 | Fat: 2g | Carbs: 47g | Protein: 9g

Bread Machine Function: Not applicable, bake in the oven.

Tortillas

Prep: 20 mins | Cook: 10 mins | Serves: 12 tortillas

Ingredients:
- **US:** 2 cups allpurpose flour, 1/2 teaspoon salt, 3/4 cup warm water, 3 tablespoons vegetable oil
- **UK:** 250g allpurpose flour, 3g salt, 180ml warm water, 45ml vegetable oil

Instructions:
1. In a large mixing bowl, combine allpurpose flour and salt.
2. Add warm water and vegetable oil to the flour mixture.
3. Stir until a dough forms.
4. Turn the dough out onto a lightly floured surface and knead for about 5 minutes until smooth.
5. Divide the dough into 12 equal portions and shape each portion into a ball.
6. Cover the dough balls with a clean kitchen towel and let them rest for about 10 minutes.
7. Preheat a skillet or griddle over mediumhigh heat.
8. Roll out each dough ball into a thin circle, about 68 inches in diameter.
9. Carefully transfer the rolledout tortilla onto the hot skillet or griddle.
10. Cook each tortilla for about 30 seconds to 1 minute on each side until lightly browned and bubbles start to form.
11. Stack the cooked tortillas on a plate and cover with a towel to keep them warm.
12. Repeat the process with the remaining dough balls.
13. Serve warm and enjoy as desired, such as for tacos, quesadillas, or wraps.

Nutritional Info: Calories: 100 | Fat: 3g | Carbs: 15g | Protein: 2g

Bread Machine Function: Not applicable, cook on a skillet or griddle.

English Muffins

Prep: 20 mins | Cook: 20 mins | Serves: 12 muffins

Ingredients:

US: 1 cup warm milk, 2 1/4 teaspoons active dry yeast, 1 tablespoon sugar, 3 cups bread flour, 1 teaspoon salt, 1 tablespoon butter, cornmeal (for dusting)

UK: 240ml warm milk, 7g active dry yeast, 15ml sugar, 375g bread flour, 5g salt, 15ml butter, cornmeal (for dusting)

Instructions:

1. In a bowl, combine warm milk, active dry yeast, and sugar. Let it sit for about 5 minutes until frothy.
2. In a large bowl, mix bread flour and salt.
3. Pour the yeast mixture into the flour mixture and stir until it forms a dough.
4. Knead the dough on a floured surface for about 10 minutes until smooth and elastic.
5. Divide the dough into 12 equal portions and shape each portion into a ball.
6. Flatten each ball slightly to form a disc shape.
7. Place the shaped muffins on a parchmentlined baking sheet dusted with cornmeal.
8. Cover the muffins with a clean towel and let them rise for about 30 minutes.
9. Preheat a skillet or griddle over medium heat and melt butter.
10. Cook the muffins for about 78 minutes on each side until golden brown and cooked through.
11. Allow the muffins to cool before slicing and toasting.

Nutritional Info: Calories: 160 | Fat: 2g | Carbs: 29g | Protein: 5g

Bread Machine Function: Not applicable, cook on a skillet or griddle.

Flatbread

Prep: 15 mins | Cook: 10 mins | Serves: 4 flatbreads

Ingredients:
- **US:** 2 cups allpurpose flour, 1 teaspoon salt, 1 tablespoon olive oil, 3/4 cup warm water
- **UK:** 250g allpurpose flour, 5g salt, 15ml olive oil, 180ml warm water

Instructions:
1. In a bowl, combine allpurpose flour and salt.
2. Add olive oil and warm water to the flour mixture.
3. Stir until a dough forms.
4. Turn the dough out onto a floured surface and knead for about 5 minutes until smooth.
5. Divide the dough into 4 equal portions and shape each portion into a ball.
6. Roll out each ball into a thin circle.
7. Heat a skillet over mediumhigh heat.
8. Cook each flatbread for 23 minutes on each side until lightly browned and cooked through.
9. Serve warm.

Nutritional Info: Calories: 180 | Fat: 3g | Carbs: 34g | Protein: 5g

Bread Machine Function: Not applicable, cook on a skillet.

CHAPTER SIX: BREADS WITH MIXINS

Cheese Bread

Prep: 10 mins | Cook: 3 hours | Serves: 1 loaf

Ingredients:
- **US:** 1 cup shredded cheddar cheese, 3 cups bread flour, 1 teaspoon salt, 1 tablespoon sugar, 1 tablespoon butter, 1 cup warm water, 2 teaspoons active dry yeast
- **UK:** 120g shredded cheddar cheese, 375g bread flour, 5g salt, 12g sugar, 14g butter, 240ml warm water, 7g active dry yeast

Instructions:
1. Add warm water, sugar, and yeast to the bread machine pan. Let it sit for 5 minutes until foamy.
2. Add bread flour, salt, and butter to the pan.
3. Select the "Basic" or "White Bread" cycle and start the machine.
4. When the machine beeps during the kneading cycle, add shredded cheddar cheese.
5. Let the bread machine complete the cycle.
6. Once done, carefully remove the bread from the pan and let it cool on a wire rack.
7. Slice and serve warm. Enjoy the cheesy goodness!

Nutritional Info: Calories: 250 | Fat: 6g | Carbs: 40g | Protein: 10g

Bread Machine Function: Basic or White Bread cycle.

Herb Bread

Prep: 10 mins | Cook: 3 hours | Serves: 1 loaf

Ingredients:
- **US:** 3 cups bread flour, 1 teaspoon salt, 1 tablespoon sugar, 1 tablespoon dried herbs (such as rosemary, thyme, or oregano), 1 tablespoon olive oil, 1 cup warm water, 2 teaspoons active dry yeast
- **UK:** 375g bread flour, 5g salt, 12g sugar, 5g dried herbs, 14g olive oil, 240ml warm water, 7g active dry yeast

Instructions:
1. Add warm water, sugar, and yeast to the bread machine pan. Let it sit for 5 minutes until foamy.
2. Add bread flour, salt, dried herbs, and olive oil to the pan.
3. Select the "Basic" or "White Bread" cycle and start the machine.
4. Let the bread machine complete the cycle.
5. Once done, carefully remove the bread from the pan and let it cool on a wire rack.
6. Slice and serve with butter for a delightful herby treat!

Nutritional Info: Calories: 230 | Fat: 3g | Carbs: 44g | Protein: 7g

Bread Machine Function: Basic or White Bread cycle.

Olive Bread

Prep: 10 mins | Cook: 3 hours | Serves: 1 loaf

Ingredients:
- **US:** 3 cups bread flour, 1 teaspoon salt, 1 tablespoon sugar, 1/2 cup sliced olives (green or black), 1 tablespoon olive oil, 1 cup warm water, 2 teaspoons active dry yeast
- **UK:** 375g bread flour, 5g salt, 12g sugar, 80g sliced olives, 14g olive oil, 240ml warm water, 7g active dry yeast

Instructions:
1. Add warm water, sugar, and yeast to the bread machine pan. Let it sit for 5 minutes until foamy.
2. Add bread flour, salt, sliced olives, and olive oil to the pan.
3. Select the "Basic" or "White Bread" cycle and start the machine.
4. Let the bread machine complete the cycle.
5. Once done, carefully remove the bread from the pan and let it cool on a wire rack.
6. Slice and serve with a Mediterranean twist!

Nutritional Info: Calories: 220 | Fat: 4g | Carbs: 42g | Protein: 6g

Bread Machine Function: Basic or White Bread cycle.

Garlic Bread

Prep: 10 mins | Cook: 3 hours | Serves: 1 loaf

Ingredients:
- **US:** 3 cups bread flour, 1 teaspoon salt, 1 tablespoon sugar, 3 cloves garlic (minced), 1 tablespoon butter (melted), 1 cup warm water, 2 teaspoons active dry yeast
- **UK:** 375g bread flour, 5g salt, 12g sugar, 3 cloves garlic (minced), 14g butter (melted), 240ml warm water, 7g active dry yeast

Instructions:
1. Add warm water, sugar, and yeast to the bread machine pan. Let it sit for 5 minutes until foamy.
2. Add bread flour, salt, minced garlic, and melted butter to the pan.
3. Select the "Basic" or "White Bread" cycle and start the machine.
4. Let the bread machine complete the cycle.
5. Once done, carefully remove the bread from the pan and let it cool on a wire rack.
6. Slice and serve with a bold garlic flavor!

Nutritional Info: Calories: 240 | Fat: 3g | Carbs: 46g | Protein: 8g

Bread Machine Function: Basic or White Bread cycle.

Onion Bread

Prep: 10 mins | Cook: 3 hours | Serves: 1 loaf

Ingredients:
- **US:** 3 cups bread flour, 1 teaspoon salt, 1 tablespoon sugar, 1/2 cup chopped onions, 1 tablespoon olive oil, 1 cup warm water, 2 teaspoons active dry yeast
- **UK:** 375g bread flour, 5g salt, 12g sugar, 80g chopped onions, 14g olive oil, 240ml warm water, 7g active dry yeast

Instructions:
1. Add warm water, sugar, and yeast to the bread machine pan. Let it sit for 5 minutes until foamy.
2. Add bread flour, salt, chopped onions, and olive oil to the pan.
3. Select the "Basic" or "White Bread" cycle and start the machine.
4. Let the bread machine complete the cycle.
5. Once done, carefully remove the bread from the pan and let it cool on a wire rack.
6. Slice and serve with the savory goodness of onions!

Nutritional Info: Calories: 230 | Fat: 4g | Carbs: 42g | Protein: 6g

Bread Machine Function: Basic or White Bread cycle.

Bacon Bread

Prep: 10 mins | Cook: 3 hours | Serves: 1 loaf

Ingredients:
- **US:** 2 cups bread flour, 1 cup cooked and crumbled bacon, 1 teaspoon salt, 1 tablespoon sugar, 1 tablespoon butter, 1 cup warm water, 2 teaspoons active dry yeast
- **UK:** 250g bread flour, 100g cooked and crumbled bacon, 5g salt, 12g sugar, 14g butter, 240ml warm water, 7g active dry yeast

Instructions:
1. Add warm water, sugar, and yeast to the bread machine pan. Let it sit for 5 minutes until foamy.
2. Add bread flour, crumbled bacon, salt, and butter to the pan.
3. Select the "Basic" or "White Bread" cycle and start the machine.
4. Let the bread machine complete the cycle.
5. Once done, carefully remove the bread from the pan and let it cool on a wire rack.
6. Slice and enjoy the smoky flavor of bacon in every bite!

Nutritional Info: Calories: 260 | Fat: 6g | Carbs: 45g | Protein: 9g

Bread Machine Function: Basic or White Bread cycle.

Jalapeno Bread

Prep: 10 mins | Cook: 3 hours | Serves: 1 loaf

Ingredients:
- **US:** 3 cups bread flour, 1 teaspoon salt, 1 tablespoon sugar, 1/4 cup chopped pickled jalapenos, 1 tablespoon olive oil, 1 cup warm water, 2 teaspoons active dry yeast
- **UK:** 375g bread flour, 5g salt, 12g sugar, 40g chopped pickled jalapenos, 14g olive oil, 240ml warm water, 7g active dry yeast

Instructions:
1. Add warm water, sugar, and yeast to the bread machine pan. Let it sit for 5 minutes until foamy.
2. Add bread flour, salt, chopped pickled jalapenos, and olive oil to the pan.
3. Select the "Basic" or "White Bread" cycle and start the machine.
4. Let the bread machine complete the cycle.
5. Once done, carefully remove the bread from the pan and let it cool on a wire rack.
6. Slice and enjoy the spicy kick of jalapenos!

Nutritional Info: Calories: 240 | Fat: 3g | Carbs: 46g | Protein: 8g

Bread Machine Function: Basic or White Bread cycle.

Dried Fruit Bread

Prep: 10 mins | Cook: 3 hours | Serves: 1 loaf

Ingredients:
- **US:** 3 cups bread flour, 1 teaspoon salt, 1 tablespoon sugar, 1/2 cup mixed dried fruits (such as raisins, cranberries, and apricots), 1 tablespoon butter, 1 cup warm water, 2 teaspoons active dry yeast
- **UK:** 375g bread flour, 5g salt, 12g sugar, 80g mixed dried fruits, 14g butter, 240ml warm water, 7g active dry yeast

Instructions:
1. Add warm water, sugar, and yeast to the bread machine pan. Let it sit for 5 minutes until foamy.
2. Add bread flour, salt, mixed dried fruits, and butter to the pan.
3. Select the "Basic" or "White Bread" cycle and start the machine.
4. Let the bread machine complete the cycle.
5. Once done, carefully remove the bread from the pan and let it cool on a wire rack.
6. Slice and enjoy the sweet and chewy bites of dried fruits!

Nutritional Info: Calories: 230 | Fat: 3g | Carbs: 45g | Protein: 7g

Bread Machine Function: Basic or White Bread cycle.

Walnut Bread

Prep: 10 mins | Cook: 3 hours | Serves: 1 loaf

Ingredients:
- **US:** 3 cups bread flour, 1 teaspoon salt, 1 tablespoon sugar, 1/2 cup chopped walnuts, 1 tablespoon olive oil, 1 cup warm water, 2 teaspoons active dry yeast
- **UK:** 375g bread flour, 5g salt, 12g sugar, 80g chopped walnuts, 14g olive oil, 240ml warm water, 7g active dry yeast

Instructions:
1. Add warm water, sugar, and yeast to the bread machine pan. Let it sit for 5 minutes until foamy.
2. Add bread flour, salt, chopped walnuts, and olive oil to the pan.
3. Select the "Basic" or "White Bread" cycle and start the machine.
4. Let the bread machine complete the cycle.
5. Once done, carefully remove the bread from the pan and let it cool on a wire rack.
6. Slice and enjoy the crunchy texture of walnuts in every bite!

Nutritional Info: Calories: 240 | Fat: 4g | Carbs: 45g | Protein: 8g

Bread Machine Function: Basic or White Bread cycle.

Cranberry Bread

Prep: 10 mins | Cook: 3 hours | Serves: 1 loaf

Ingredients:
- **US:** 3 cups bread flour, 1 teaspoon salt, 1 tablespoon sugar, 1/2 cup dried cranberries, 1 tablespoon butter, 1 cup warm water, 2 teaspoons active dry yeast
- **UK:** 375g bread flour, 5g salt, 12g sugar, 80g dried cranberries, 14g butter, 240ml warm water, 7g active dry yeast

Instructions:
1. Add warm water, sugar, and yeast to the bread machine pan. Let it sit for 5 minutes until foamy.
2. Add bread flour, salt, dried cranberries, and butter to the pan.
3. Select the "Basic" or "White Bread" cycle and start the machine.
4. Let the bread machine complete the cycle.
5. Once done, carefully remove the bread from the pan and let it cool on a wire rack.
6. Slice and enjoy the burst of tartness from cranberries!

Nutritional Info: Calories: 230 | Fat: 3g | Carbs: 45g | Protein: 7g

Bread Machine Function: Basic or White Bread cycle.

Cheddar Bread

Prep: 10 mins | Cook: 3 hours | Serves: 1 loaf

Ingredients:
- **US:** 3 cups bread flour, 1 teaspoon salt, 1 tablespoon sugar, 1 cup shredded cheddar cheese, 1 tablespoon olive oil, 1 cup warm water, 2 teaspoons active dry yeast
- **UK:** 375g bread flour, 5g salt, 12g sugar, 120g shredded cheddar cheese, 14g olive oil, 240ml warm water, 7g active dry yeast

Instructions:
1. Add warm water, sugar, and yeast to the bread machine pan. Let it sit for 5 minutes until foamy.
2. Add bread flour, salt, shredded cheddar cheese, and olive oil to the pan.
3. Select the "Basic" or "White Bread" cycle and start the machine.
4. Let the bread machine complete the cycle.
5. Once done, carefully remove the bread from the pan and let it cool on a wire rack.
6. Slice and enjoy the cheesy goodness of cheddar bread!

Nutritional Info: Calories: 250 | Fat: 5g | Carbs: 40g | Protein: 10g

Bread Machine Function: Basic or White Bread cycle.

Feta Bread

Prep: 10 mins | Cook: 3 hours | Serves: 1 loaf

Ingredients:
- **US:** 3 cups bread flour, 1 teaspoon salt, 1 tablespoon sugar, 1/2 cup crumbled feta cheese, 1 tablespoon olive oil, 1 cup warm water, 2 teaspoons active dry yeast
- **UK:** 375g bread flour, 5g salt, 12g sugar, 80g crumbled feta cheese, 14g olive oil, 240ml warm water, 7g active dry yeast

Instructions:
1. Add warm water, sugar, and yeast to the bread machine pan. Let it sit for 5 minutes until foamy.
2. Add bread flour, salt, crumbled feta cheese, and olive oil to the pan.
3. Select the "Basic" or "White Bread" cycle and start the machine.
4. Let the bread machine complete the cycle.
5. Once done, carefully remove the bread from the pan and let it cool on a wire rack.
6. Slice and enjoy the tangy flavor of feta cheese!

Nutritional Info: Calories: 230 | Fat: 4g | Carbs: 44g | Protein: 8g

Bread Machine Function: Basic or White Bread cycle.

Sundried Tomato Bread

Prep: 10 mins | Cook: 3 hours | Serves: 1 loaf

Ingredients:
- **US:** 3 cups bread flour, 1 teaspoon salt, 1 tablespoon sugar, 1/2 cup chopped sundried tomatoes, 1 tablespoon olive oil, 1 cup warm water, 2 teaspoons active dry yeast
- **UK:** 375g bread flour, 5g salt, 12g sugar, 80g chopped sundried tomatoes, 14g olive oil, 240ml warm water, 7g active dry yeast

Instructions:
1. Add warm water, sugar, and yeast to the bread machine pan. Let it sit for 5 minutes until foamy.
2. Add bread flour, salt, chopped sundried tomatoes, and olive oil to the pan.
3. Select the "Basic" or "White Bread" cycle and start the machine.
4. Let the bread machine complete the cycle.
5. Once done, carefully remove the bread from the pan and let it cool on a wire rack.
6. Slice and enjoy the savory taste of sundried tomatoes!

Nutritional Info: Calories: 240 | Fat: 3g | Carbs: 46g | Protein: 8g

Bread Machine Function: Basic or White Bread cycle.

Rosemary Bread

Prep: 10 mins | Cook: 3 hours | Serves: 1 loaf

Ingredients:

US: 3 cups bread flour, 1 teaspoon salt, 1 tablespoon sugar, 1 tablespoon chopped fresh rosemary, 1 tablespoon olive oil, 1 cup warm water, 2 teaspoons active dry yeast

UK: 375g bread flour, 5g salt, 12g sugar, 5g chopped fresh rosemary, 14g olive oil, 240ml warm water, 7g active dry yeast

Instructions:
1. Add warm water, sugar, and yeast to the bread machine pan. Let it sit for 5 minutes until foamy.
2. Add bread flour, salt, chopped fresh rosemary, and olive oil to the pan.
3. Select the "Basic" or "White Bread" cycle and start the machine.
4. Let the bread machine complete the cycle.
5. Once done, carefully remove the bread from the pan and let it cool on a wire rack.
6. Slice and enjoy the fragrant aroma of rosemary in every bite!

Nutritional Info: Calories: 230 | Fat: 4g | Carbs: 42g | Protein: 7g

Bread Machine Function: Basic or White Bread cycle.

Pesto Bread

Prep: 10 mins | Cook: 3 hours | Serves: 1 loaf

Ingredients:
- **US:** 3 cups bread flour, 1 teaspoon salt, 1 tablespoon sugar, 2 tablespoons pesto sauce, 1 tablespoon olive oil, 1 cup warm water, 2 teaspoons active dry yeast
- **UK:** 375g bread flour, 5g salt, 12g sugar, 30g pesto sauce, 14g olive oil, 240ml warm water, 7g active dry yeast

Instructions:
1. Add warm water, sugar, and yeast to the bread machine pan. Let it sit for 5 minutes until foamy.
2. Add bread flour, salt, pesto sauce, and olive oil to the pan.
3. Select the "Basic" or "White Bread" cycle and start the machine.
4. Let the bread machine complete the cycle.
5. Once done, carefully remove the bread from the pan and let it cool on a wire rack.
6. Slice and enjoy the vibrant flavor of pesto in every slice!

Nutritional Info: Calories: 240 | Fat: 4g | Carbs: 45g | Protein: 8g

Bread Machine Function: Basic or White Bread cycle.

Spinach Bread

Prep: 10 mins | Cook: 3 hours | Serves: 1 loaf

Ingredients:
- **US:** 3 cups bread flour, 1 teaspoon salt, 1 tablespoon sugar, 1/2 cup chopped spinach, 1 tablespoon olive oil, 1 cup warm water, 2 teaspoons active dry yeast
- **UK:** 375g bread flour, 5g salt, 12g sugar, 80g chopped spinach, 14g olive oil, 240ml warm water, 7g active dry yeast

Instructions:
1. Add warm water, sugar, and yeast to the bread machine pan. Let it sit for 5 minutes until foamy.
2. Add bread flour, salt, chopped spinach, and olive oil to the pan.
3. Select the "Basic" or "White Bread" cycle and start the machine.
4. Let the bread machine complete the cycle.
5. Once done, carefully remove the bread from the pan and let it cool on a wire rack.
6. Slice and enjoy the earthy flavor of spinach in each bite!

Nutritional Info: Calories: 230 | Fat: 4g | Carbs: 42g | Protein: 7g

Bread Machine Function: Basic or White Bread cycle.

Caramelized Onion Bread

Prep: 10 mins | Cook: 3 hours | Serves: 1 loaf

Ingredients:
- **US:** 3 cups bread flour, 1 teaspoon salt, 1 tablespoon sugar, 1/2 cup caramelized onions, 1 tablespoon butter, 1 cup warm water, 2 teaspoons active dry yeast
- **UK:** 375g bread flour, 5g salt, 12g sugar, 80g caramelized onions, 14g butter, 240ml warm water, 7g active dry yeast

Instructions:
1. Add warm water, sugar, and yeast to the bread machine pan. Let it sit for 5 minutes until foamy.
2. Add bread flour, salt, caramelized onions, and butter to the pan.
3. Select the "Basic" or "White Bread" cycle and start the machine.
4. Let the bread machine complete the cycle.
5. Once done, carefully remove the bread from the pan and let it cool on a wire rack.
6. Slice and enjoy the sweet and savory taste of caramelized onions!

Nutritional Info: Calories: 240 | Fat: 4g | Carbs: 45g | Protein: 7g

Bread Machine Function: Basic or White Bread cycle.

Raisin Bread

Prep: 10 mins | Cook: 3 hours | Serves: 1 loaf

Ingredients:
- **US:** 3 cups bread flour, 1 teaspoon salt, 1 tablespoon sugar, 1/2 cup raisins, 1 tablespoon butter, 1 cup warm water, 2 teaspoons active dry yeast
- **UK:** 375g bread flour, 5g salt, 12g sugar, 80g raisins, 14g butter, 240ml warm water, 7g active dry yeast

Instructions:
1. Add warm water, sugar, and yeast to the bread machine pan. Let it sit for 5 minutes until foamy.
2. Add bread flour, salt, raisins, and butter to the pan.
3. Select the "Basic" or "White Bread" cycle and start the machine.
4. Let the bread machine complete the cycle.
5. Once done, carefully remove the bread from the pan and let it cool on a wire rack.
6. Slice and enjoy the sweet and chewy bites of raisin bread!

Nutritional Info: Calories: 230 | Fat: 4g | Carbs: 42g | Protein: 7g

Bread Machine Function: Basic or White Bread cycle.

CHAPTER SEVEN: ARTISAN BREADS

Sourdough Bread

Prep: 15 mins | Cook: 3 hours | Serves: 1 loaf

Ingredients:
- **US:** 2 cups bread flour, 1 cup sourdough starter, 1 teaspoon salt, 1 tablespoon honey, 1 tablespoon olive oil, 1/2 cup warm water, 2 teaspoons active dry yeast
- **UK:** 250g bread flour, 240g sourdough starter, 5g salt, 15g honey, 14g olive oil, 120ml warm water, 7g active dry yeast

Instructions:
1. In the bread machine pan, combine warm water, honey, and yeast. Let it sit for 5 minutes until foamy.
2. Add sourdough starter, bread flour, salt, and olive oil to the pan.
3. Select the "Sourdough" or "Artisan" cycle and start the machine.
4. Allow the bread machine to complete the cycle, including fermentation time.
5. Once done, carefully remove the sourdough bread from the pan and let it cool on a wire rack.
6. Slice and enjoy the tangy flavor of homemade sourdough bread!

Nutritional Info: Calories: 200 | Fat: 2g | Carbs: 40g | Protein: 6g

Bread Machine Function: Sourdough or Artisan cycle.

Ciabatta

Prep: 15 mins | Cook: 3 hours | Serves: 1 loaf

Ingredients:
- **US:** 2 1/2 cups bread flour, 1 teaspoon salt, 1 teaspoon sugar, 1 tablespoon olive oil, 1 cup warm water, 2 teaspoons active dry yeast
- **UK:** 310g bread flour, 5g salt, 5g sugar, 14g olive oil, 240ml warm water, 7g active dry yeast

Instructions:
1. Combine warm water, sugar, and yeast in the bread machine pan. Let it sit for 5 minutes until frothy.
2. Add bread flour, salt, and olive oil to the pan.
3. Select the "Dough" or "Pizza Dough" cycle and start the machine.
4. Once the dough cycle is complete, remove the dough from the machine and shape it into a ciabatta loaf on a floured surface.
5. Preheat the oven to 425°F (220°C).
6. Place the shaped ciabatta dough on a baking sheet lined with parchment paper and let it rise for 30 minutes.
7. Bake the ciabatta in the preheated oven for 2025 minutes until golden brown.
8. Allow the ciabatta to cool on a wire rack before slicing and serving.

Nutritional Info: Calories: 180 | Fat: 3g | Carbs: 35g | Protein: 5g

Bread Machine Function: Dough or Pizza Dough cycle.

Focaccia

Prep: 15 mins | Cook: 2 hours | Serves: 1 loaf

Ingredients:
- **US:** 3 cups bread flour, 1 teaspoon salt, 1 tablespoon sugar, 1 tablespoon olive oil, 1 cup warm water, 2 teaspoons active dry yeast, 2 tablespoons fresh rosemary (chopped), 2 cloves garlic (minced), coarse salt for sprinkling
- **UK:** 375g bread flour, 5g salt, 15g sugar, 14g olive oil, 240ml warm water, 7g active dry yeast, 30g fresh rosemary (chopped), 2 cloves garlic (minced), coarse salt for sprinkling

Instructions:
1. In the bread machine pan, combine warm water, sugar, and yeast. Let it sit for 5 minutes until frothy.
2. Add bread flour, salt, and olive oil to the pan. Select the "Dough" or "Pizza Dough" cycle and start the machine.
3. Once the dough cycle is complete, remove the dough from the machine and press it into a greased baking sheet.
4. Cover the dough with a clean kitchen towel and let it rise for 3045 minutes.
5. Preheat the oven to 400°F (200°C).
6. After rising, use your fingers to create dimples in the dough. Brush the top with olive oil and sprinkle chopped rosemary, minced garlic, and coarse salt.
7. Bake the focaccia in the preheated oven for 2025 minutes until golden brown.
8. Allow the focaccia to cool slightly before slicing and serving.

Nutritional Info: Calories: 220 | Fat: 4g | Carbs: 40g | Protein: 6g

Bread Machine Function: Dough or Pizza Dough cycle.

Baguettes

Prep: 15 mins | Cook: 25 mins | Serves: 2 baguettes

Ingredients:
- **US:** 3 cups bread flour, 1 1/4 cups water, 2 teaspoons salt, 1 teaspoon sugar, 2 teaspoons active dry yeast
- **UK:** 375g bread flour, 300ml water, 10g salt, 5g sugar, 7g active dry yeast

Instructions:
1. Add water, sugar, and yeast to the bread machine pan. Let it sit for 5 minutes until frothy.
2. Add bread flour and salt to the pan. Select the "Dough" or "French Bread" cycle and start the machine.
3. Once the dough cycle is complete, divide the dough into two equal portions.
4. Shape each portion into a baguette shape and place them on a greased or parchmentlined baking sheet.
5. Cover the baguettes with a clean kitchen towel and let them rise for 3045 minutes.
6. Preheat the oven to 450°F (230°C).
7. Make diagonal slashes on the top of each baguette with a sharp knife.
8. Bake the baguettes in the preheated oven for 2025 minutes until golden brown and hollowsounding when tapped on the bottom.
9. Allow the baguettes to cool on a wire rack before slicing and serving.

Nutritional Info: Calories: 180 | Fat: 1g | Carbs: 35g | Protein: 6g

Bread Machine Function: Dough or French Bread cycle.

Batards

Prep: 15 mins | Cook: 25 mins | Serves: 2 batards

Ingredients:
- **US:** 3 cups bread flour, 1 1/4 cups water, 2 teaspoons salt, 1 teaspoon sugar, 2 teaspoons active dry yeast
- **UK:** 375g bread flour, 300ml water, 10g salt, 5g sugar, 7g active dry yeast

Instructions:
1. Follow the same instructions as for Baguettes, shaping the dough into batard shapes instead.
2. Batards are shorter and thicker than baguettes, resembling oval loaves. Follow the same baking instructions.

Nutritional Info: Calories: 180 | Fat: 1g | Carbs: 35g | Protein: 6g

Bread Machine Function: Dough or French Bread cycle.

Boules

Prep: 15 mins | Cook: 35 mins | Serves: 1 large loaf

Ingredients:
- **US:** 3 cups bread flour, 1 1/4 cups warm water, 2 teaspoons active dry yeast, 1 teaspoon salt, 1 tablespoon olive oil
- **UK:** 375g bread flour, 300ml warm water, 7g active dry yeast, 5g salt, 15ml olive oil

Instructions:
1. In the bread machine pan, combine the warm water and yeast. Let it sit for 510 minutes until foamy.
2. Add the bread flour, salt, and olive oil to the pan. Select the "Dough" or "Manual" cycle and start the machine.
3. Once the dough cycle is complete, turn the dough out onto a floured surface. Shape it into a round boule.
4. Place the boule on a baking sheet lined with parchment paper. Cover it with a clean kitchen towel and let it rise in a warm place for about 3045 minutes.
5. Preheat the oven to 450°F (230°C).
6. Slash the top of the boule with a sharp knife to create decorative patterns.
7. Bake the boule for 3035 minutes, or until the crust is deep golden brown and the loaf sounds hollow when tapped on the bottom.
8. Allow the bread to cool on a wire rack before slicing and serving.

Nutritional Info: Calories: 210 | Fat: 3g | Carbs: 40g | Protein: 6g

Bread Machine Function: Dough cycle.

Rye Bread

Prep: 10 mins | Cook: 3 hours | Serves: 1 loaf

Ingredients:
- **US:** 2 cups rye flour, 1 cup bread flour, 1 1/4 cups water, 2 tablespoons molasses, 1 1/2 tablespoons vegetable oil, 1 1/2 teaspoons salt, 2 teaspoons caraway seeds, 2 teaspoons active dry yeast
- **UK:** 250g rye flour, 125g bread flour, 300ml water, 30ml molasses, 22ml vegetable oil, 10g salt, 7g caraway seeds, 7g active dry yeast

Instructions:
1. Place all ingredients in the bread machine pan according to the manufacturer's instructions.
2. Select the "Basic" or "Whole Wheat" cycle, depending on your machine's options.

3. Start the bread machine and let it complete the cycle.
4. Once done, remove the bread from the pan and let it cool on a wire rack before slicing.

Nutritional Info: Calories: 170 | Fat: 3g | Carbs: 32g | Protein: 4g

Bread Machine Function: Basic or Whole Wheat cycle.

Pumpernickel Bread

Prep: 15 mins | Cook: 3 hours | Serves: 1 loaf

Ingredients:
- **US:** 1 1/2 cups rye flour, 1 1/2 cups bread flour, 1/2 cup cornmeal, 1 1/4 cups water, 2 tablespoons molasses, 1 1/2 tablespoons vegetable oil, 1 1/2 teaspoons salt, 2 teaspoons cocoa powder, 2 teaspoons caraway seeds, 2 teaspoons active dry yeast
- **UK:** 190g rye flour, 190g bread flour, 65g cornmeal, 300ml water, 30ml molasses, 22ml vegetable oil, 10g salt, 4g cocoa powder, 7g caraway seeds, 7g active dry yeast

1. *Instructions:*
1. Add all ingredients to the bread machine pan in the order recommended by the manufacturer.
2. Select the "Whole Wheat" or "Multigrain" cycle, if available.
3. Start the bread machine and allow it to complete the cycle.
4. Once finished, remove the loaf from the pan and let it cool on a wire rack before slicing.

Nutritional Info: Calories: 180 | Fat: 3g | Carbs: 33g | Protein: 4g

Bread Machine Function: Whole Wheat or Multigrain cycle.

Multigrain Bread

Prep: 15 mins | Cook: 3 hours | Serves: 1 loaf

Ingredients:
- **US:** 1 1/2 cups bread flour, 1 cup whole wheat flour, 1/2 cup oats, 1/4 cup cornmeal, 1/4 cup flaxseeds, 1 1/4 cups water, 2 tablespoons honey, 2 tablespoons olive oil, 1 1/2 teaspoons salt, 2 teaspoons active dry yeast
- **UK:** 190g bread flour, 125g whole wheat flour, 65g oats, 30g cornmeal, 30g flaxseeds, 300ml water, 30ml honey, 30ml olive oil, 10g salt, 7g active dry yeast

Instructions:
1. Place all ingredients in the bread machine pan according to the manufacturer's instructions.
2. Select the "Whole Wheat" or "Multigrain" cycle and start the machine.
3. Once the cycle is complete, remove the bread from the machine and let it cool before slicing.

Nutritional Info: Calories: 190 | Fat: 4g | Carbs: 35g | Protein: 5g

Bread Machine Function: Whole Wheat or Multigrain cycle.

Semmel Rolls

Prep: 15 mins | Cook: 3 hours | Serves: 1 dozen rolls

Ingredients:
- **US:** 3 cups bread flour, 1 cup water, 2 tablespoons unsalted butter (softened), 2 tablespoons granulated sugar, 1 1/2 teaspoons salt, 2 teaspoons active dry yeast, 1 egg (beaten, for egg wash)
- **UK:** 375g bread flour, 240ml water, 30g unsalted butter (softened), 25g granulated sugar, 10g salt, 7g active dry yeast, 1 egg (beaten, for egg wash)

Instructions:
1. Add all ingredients (except the egg wash) to the bread machine pan in the order recommended by the manufacturer.
2. Select the "Dough" or "Manual" cycle and start the machine.
3. Once the dough cycle is complete, divide the dough into 12 equal pieces and shape them into rolls.
4. Place the rolls on a baking sheet lined with parchment paper, cover with a clean kitchen towel, and let them rise in a warm place for about 30 minutes.
5. Preheat the oven to 375°F (190°C). Brush the risen rolls with the beaten egg.
6. Bake the rolls for 1518 minutes or until they are golden brown.
7. Remove from the oven and let cool on a wire rack before serving.

Nutritional Info: Calories: 160 | Fat: 3g | Carbs: 28g | Protein: 5g

Bread Machine Function: Dough cycle.

Pretzels

Prep: 20 mins | Cook: 15 mins | Serves: 8 pretzels

Ingredients:
- **US:** 2 cups bread flour, 1/2 cup warm water, 1 tablespoon granulated sugar, 1 teaspoon salt, 2 teaspoons active dry yeast, 1/4 cup baking soda, coarse salt (for topping), 1 egg (beaten, for egg wash)
- **UK:** 250g bread flour, 120ml warm water, 15g granulated sugar, 5g salt, 7g active dry yeast, 60g baking soda, coarse salt (for topping), 1 egg (beaten, for egg wash)

Instructions:
1. Add the warm water, sugar, salt, and yeast to the bread machine pan. Let it sit for 510 minutes until foamy.
2. Add the bread flour to the pan and select the "Dough" or "Manual" cycle. Start the machine.
3. Once the dough cycle is complete, preheat the oven to 425°F (220°C) and line a baking sheet with parchment paper.

4. Divide the dough into 8 equal pieces and roll each piece into a rope. Shape the ropes into pretzels.
5. In a shallow dish, dissolve the baking soda in warm water. Dip each pretzel into the baking soda solution and place them on the prepared baking sheet.
6. Brush the pretzels with beaten egg and sprinkle with coarse salt.
7. Bake for 1215 minutes or until golden brown.
8. Let the pretzels cool slightly before serving.

Nutritional Info: Calories: 150 | Fat: 1g | Carbs: 29g | Protein: 5g

Bread Machine Function: Dough cycle.

Bagels

Prep: 20 mins | Cook: 20 mins | Serves: 8 bagels

Ingredients:
- **US:** 3 cups bread flour, 1 cup warm water, 2 tablespoons granulated sugar, 1 1/2 teaspoons salt, 2 teaspoons active dry yeast, 1 egg (beaten, for egg wash), toppings of choice (e.g., sesame seeds, poppy seeds)
- **UK:** 375g bread flour, 240ml warm water, 25g granulated sugar, 10g salt, 7g active dry yeast, 1 egg (beaten, for egg wash), toppings of choice (e.g., sesame seeds, poppy seeds)

Instructions:
1. Add the warm water, sugar, salt, and yeast to the bread machine pan. Let it sit for 510 minutes until foamy.
2. Add the bread flour to the pan and select the "Dough" or "Manual" cycle. Start the machine.
3. Once the dough cycle is complete, divide the dough into 8 equal pieces. Roll each piece into a ball, then flatten slightly to form a bagel shape.
4. Preheat the oven to 425°F (220°C) and line a baking sheet with parchment paper.
5. Bring a large pot of water to a boil. Carefully drop the bagels into the boiling water and boil for 1 minute on each side.

6. Remove the bagels from the water using a slotted spoon and place them on the prepared baking sheet.
7. Brush the bagels with beaten egg and sprinkle with toppings of your choice.
8. Bake for 1820 minutes or until the bagels are golden brown.
9. Allow the bagels to cool before slicing and serving.

Nutritional Info: Calories: 200 | Fat: 1g | Carbs: 40g | Protein: 7g

Bread Machine Function: Dough cycle.

English Muffins

Prep: 15 mins | Cook: 20 mins | Serves: 8 muffins

Ingredients:
- **US:** 2 cups bread flour, 3/4 cup warm milk, 1 tablespoon granulated sugar, 1 teaspoon salt, 1 1/2 teaspoons active dry yeast, cornmeal (for dusting)
- **UK:** 250g bread flour, 180ml warm milk, 15g granulated sugar, 5g salt, 7g active dry yeast, cornmeal (for dusting)

Instructions:
1. In the bread machine pan, combine the warm milk, sugar, salt, and yeast. Let it sit for 510 minutes until foamy.
2. Add the bread flour to the pan and select the "Dough" or "Manual" cycle. Start the machine.
3. Once the dough cycle is complete, turn the dough out onto a floured surface. Roll out the dough to about 1/2 inch thickness.
4. Use a round cutter to cut out circles of dough, about 34 inches in diameter. Place the muffins on a baking sheet dusted with cornmeal.
5. Cover the muffins with a clean kitchen towel and let them rise in a warm place for about 30 minutes.
6. Heat a skillet or griddle over medium heat. Cook the muffins for about 710 minutes on each side, until golden brown and cooked through.
7. Allow the muffins to cool slightly before splitting them with a fork and toasting.

Nutritional Info: Calories: 150 | Fat: 1g | Carbs: 29g | Protein: 5g

Bread Machine Function: Dough cycle.

Croissants

Prep: 30 mins | Cook: 15 mins | Serves: 12 croissants

Ingredients:
- **US:** 2 cups bread flour, 1/4 cup warm milk, 1/4 cup cold water, 3 tablespoons granulated sugar, 1 teaspoon salt, 2 teaspoons active dry yeast, 1 cup unsalted butter (cold), 1 egg (beaten, for egg wash)
- **UK:** 250g bread flour, 60ml warm milk, 60ml cold water, 25g granulated sugar, 5g salt, 7g active dry yeast, 225g unsalted butter (cold), 1 egg (beaten, for egg wash)

Instructions:
1. In the bread machine pan, combine the warm milk, cold water, sugar, salt, and yeast. Let it sit for 510 minutes until foamy.
2. Add the bread flour to the pan and select the "Dough" or "Manual" cycle. Start the machine.
3. Once the dough cycle is complete, turn the dough out onto a floured surface. Roll out the dough into a large rectangle.
4. Place the cold butter in the center of the dough and fold the sides over to encase the butter completely. Roll out the dough again into a large rectangle.
5. Fold the dough into thirds like a letter, then roll it out again into a large rectangle. Repeat this folding process two more times, then wrap the dough in plastic wrap and refrigerate for at least 1 hour.
6. Preheat the oven to 400°F (200°C) and line a baking sheet with parchment paper.
7. Roll out the chilled dough into a large rectangle and cut it into triangles. Roll each triangle up tightly, starting from the wide end, to form a croissant shape.
8. Place the croissants on the prepared baking sheet, brush them with beaten egg, and let them rise in a warm place for about 30 minutes.
9. Bake the croissants for 1215 minutes or until golden brown and flaky.

Nutritional Info: Calories: 250 | Fat: 15g | Carbs: 24g | Protein: 5g

Bread Machine Function: Dough cycle.

Brioche

Prep: 15 mins | Cook: 3 hours | Serves: 1 loaf

Ingredients:
- **US:** 2 cups bread flour, 3 large eggs, 1/4 cup warm milk, 2 tablespoons granulated sugar, 1 teaspoon salt, 1/2 cup unsalted butter (softened), 2 teaspoons active dry yeast
- **UK:** 250g bread flour, 3 large eggs, 60ml warm milk, 25g granulated sugar, 5g salt, 115g unsalted butter (softened), 7g active dry yeast

Instructions:
1. Add all ingredients to the bread machine pan in the order recommended by the manufacturer.
2. Select the "Sweet Bread" or "Dough" cycle and start the machine.
3. Once the dough is ready, remove it from the machine and shape it into a loaf.
4. Place the dough in a greased loaf pan and cover it loosely with plastic wrap.
5. Let the dough rise in a warm place for about 12 hours, until doubled in size.
6. Preheat the oven to 350°F (180°C).
7. Bake the brioche for 2530 minutes, or until golden brown and cooked through.
8. Allow the brioche to cool in the pan for a few minutes before transferring it to a wire rack to cool completely.

Nutritional Info: Calories: 280 | Fat: 15g | Carbs: 30g | Protein: 6g

Bread Machine Function: Sweet Bread or Dough cycle.

Challah

Prep: 20 mins | Cook: 40 mins | Serves: 1 loaf

Ingredients:
- **US:** 3 1/2 cups bread flour, 1/4 cup granulated sugar, 1 teaspoon salt, 2 teaspoons active dry yeast, 3 large eggs (plus 1 for egg wash), 1/4 cup vegetable oil, 3/4 cup warm water
- **UK:** 440g bread flour, 50g granulated sugar, 5g salt, 7g active dry yeast, 3 large eggs (plus 1 for egg wash), 60ml vegetable oil, 180ml warm water

Instructions:
1. In the bread machine pan, combine the warm water, sugar, salt, and yeast. Let it sit for 510 minutes until foamy.
2. Add the eggs, vegetable oil, and bread flour to the pan. Select the "Dough" or "Manual" cycle and start the machine.
3. Once the dough cycle is complete, turn the dough out onto a floured surface. Divide it into three equal parts.
4. Roll each part into a long rope, then braid the ropes together to form a loaf.
5. Place the braided loaf on a baking sheet lined with parchment paper.
6. Cover the loaf with a clean kitchen towel and let it rise in a warm place for about 30 minutes.
7. Preheat the oven to 350°F (180°C).
8. Beat the remaining egg and brush it over the risen loaf.
9. Bake the challah for 3040 minutes, or until golden brown and cooked through.

Nutritional Info: Calories: 270 | Fat: 8g | Carbs: 42g | Protein: 8g

Bread Machine Function: Dough cycle.

Pain au Lait

Prep: 15 mins | Cook: 25 mins | Serves: 1 dozen rolls

Ingredients:
- **US:** 3 cups bread flour, 1/4 cup granulated sugar, 1 teaspoon salt, 2 teaspoons active dry yeast, 1 cup warm milk, 1/4 cup unsalted butter (softened), 1 egg
- **UK:** 375g bread flour, 50g granulated sugar, 5g salt, 7g active dry yeast, 240ml warm milk, 55g unsalted butter (softened), 1 egg

Instructions:
1. In the bread machine pan, combine the warm milk, sugar, salt, and yeast. Let it sit for 510 minutes until foamy.
2. Add the softened butter, egg, and bread flour to the pan. Select the "Dough" or "Manual" cycle and start the machine.
3. Once the dough cycle is complete, turn the dough out onto a floured surface. Divide it into 12 equal parts and shape each into a ball.
4. Place the dough balls on a baking sheet lined with parchment paper, leaving some space between each roll.
5. Cover the rolls with a clean kitchen towel and let them rise in a warm place for about 3045 minutes.
6. Preheat the oven to 375°F (190°C).
7. Bake the rolls for 2025 minutes, or until golden brown and cooked through.
8. Remove from the oven and let cool slightly before serving.

Nutritional Info: Calories: 180 | Fat: 5g | Carbs: 28g | Protein: 5g

Bread Machine Function: Dough cycle.

Pain de Campagne

Prep: 20 mins | Cook: 40 mins | Serves: 1 loaf

Ingredients:
- **US:** 2 1/2 cups bread flour, 1/2 cup whole wheat flour, 1 teaspoon salt, 1 teaspoon sugar, 2 teaspoons active dry yeast, 1 cup warm water, 2 tablespoons olive oil
- **UK:** 320g bread flour, 65g whole wheat flour, 5g salt, 5g sugar, 7g active dry yeast, 240ml warm water, 30ml olive oil

Instructions:
1. In the bread machine pan, combine the warm water, sugar, salt, and yeast. Let it sit for 510 minutes until foamy.
2. Add the olive oil, bread flour, and whole wheat flour to the pan. Select the "Basic" or "French" cycle and start the machine.
3. Once the dough cycle is complete, shape the dough into a round loaf and place it on a baking sheet lined with parchment paper.
4. Cover the loaf with a clean kitchen towel and let it rise in a warm place for about 3045 minutes.
5. Preheat the oven to 400°F (200°C).
6. Slash the top of the loaf with a sharp knife, then bake for 3040 minutes, or until the crust is golden brown and the loaf sounds hollow when tapped on the bottom.
7. Allow the bread to cool on a wire rack before slicing and serving.

Nutritional Info: Calories: 200 | Fat: 4g | Carbs: 35g | Protein: 6g

Bread Machine Function: Basic or French cycle.

CHAPTER EIGHT: INTERNATIONAL BREAD

French Bread

Prep: 15 mins | Cook: 25 mins | Serves: 1 loaf

Ingredients:
- **US:** 3 cups bread flour, 1 1/4 cups water, 2 teaspoons active dry yeast, 1 1/2 teaspoons salt
- **UK:** 375g bread flour, 300ml water, 7g active dry yeast, 7g salt

Instructions:
1. Add water to the bread machine pan, then add flour, yeast, and salt.
2. Select the "French Bread" or "Basic White" cycle and start the machine.
3. Once the cycle is complete, remove the dough and shape it into a long loaf.
4. Place the loaf on a baking sheet, cover it, and let it rise for 30 minutes.
5. Preheat the oven to 400°F (200°C).
6. Bake the bread for 25 minutes or until golden brown.

Nutritional Info: Calories: 160 | Fat: 0.5g | Carbs: 33g | Protein: 5g

Bread Machine Function: French Bread cycle.

Italian Bread

Prep: 10 mins | Cook: 30 mins | Serves: 1 loaf

Ingredients:
- **US:** 3 cups bread flour, 1 cup water, 2 teaspoons active dry yeast, 1 teaspoon salt, 1 tablespoon olive oil
- **UK:** 375g bread flour, 240ml water, 7g active dry yeast, 5g salt, 15ml olive oil

Instructions:
1. Combine water, yeast, salt, and olive oil in the bread machine pan.
2. Add flour to the pan.
3. Select the "Italian Bread" or "Basic White" cycle and start the machine.
4. Once the cycle is complete, shape the dough into a traditional Italian loaf.
5. Place the loaf on a baking sheet, cover it, and let it rise for 30 minutes.
6. Preheat the oven to 400°F (200°C).
7. Bake the bread for 2530 minutes until it's golden brown and sounds hollow when tapped.

Nutritional Info: Calories: 170 | Fat: 1g | Carbs: 33g | Protein: 5g

Bread Machine Function: Italian Bread cycle.

German Bread

Prep: 15 mins | Cook: 40 mins | Serves: 1 loaf

Ingredients:
- **US:** 2 1/2 cups bread flour, 1 cup lukewarm water, 1 tablespoon honey, 2 teaspoons active dry yeast, 1 teaspoon salt, 1 tablespoon unsalted butter
- **UK:** 310g bread flour, 240ml lukewarm water, 15ml honey, 7g active dry yeast, 5g salt, 15g unsalted butter

Instructions:
1. In the bread machine pan, combine lukewarm water, honey, yeast, and let it sit for 5 minutes until foamy.
2. Add bread flour, salt, and butter to the pan.
3. Select the "German Bread" or "Basic White" cycle and start the machine.
4. Once the cycle is complete, remove the dough and shape it into a loaf.
5. Place the loaf on a greased baking sheet, cover it, and let it rise for 30 minutes.
6. Preheat the oven to 375°F (190°C).

7. Bake the bread for 3540 minutes until it's golden brown and sounds hollow when tapped.

Nutritional Info: Calories: 180 | Fat: 2g | Carbs: 34g | Protein: 6g

Bread Machine Function: German Bread cycle.

Greek Bread

Prep: 15 mins | Cook: 25 mins | Serves: 1 loaf

Ingredients:

   US: 2 1/2 cups bread flour, 1 cup lukewarm water, 2 tablespoons olive oil, 2 teaspoons active dry yeast, 1 teaspoon salt, 1 tablespoon chopped fresh oregano

   UK: 310g bread flour, 240ml lukewarm water, 30ml olive oil, 7g active dry yeast, 5g salt, 15g chopped fresh oregano

Instructions:
1. Combine lukewarm water, olive oil, yeast, and let it sit for 5 minutes until foamy.
2. Add bread flour, salt, and chopped fresh oregano to the bread machine pan.
3. Select the "Greek Bread" or "Basic White" cycle and start the machine.
4. Once the cycle is complete, shape the dough into a round loaf.
5. Place the loaf on a baking sheet lined with parchment paper, cover it, and let it rise for 30 minutes.
6. Preheat the oven to 400°F (200°C).
7. Bake the bread for 2025 minutes until golden brown.

Nutritional Info: Calories: 160 | Fat: 3g | Carbs: 30g | Protein: 5g

Bread Machine Function: Greek Bread cycle.

Middle Eastern Bread

Prep: 10 mins | Cook: 15 mins | Serves: 6 pieces

Ingredients:
- **US:** 2 cups allpurpose flour, 1 teaspoon salt, 1 tablespoon sugar, 2 tablespoons olive oil, 1 teaspoon active dry yeast, 3/4 cup lukewarm water
- **UK:** 250g allpurpose flour, 5g salt, 12g sugar, 30ml olive oil, 7g active dry yeast, 180ml lukewarm water

Instructions:
1. In the bread machine pan, combine lukewarm water, sugar, and yeast. Let it rest for 5 minutes.
2. Add flour, salt, and olive oil to the pan.
3. Select the "Dough" cycle and start the machine.
4. Once the dough is ready, divide it into 6 equal portions and roll each into a ball.
5. On a floured surface, flatten each ball into a circle about 1/4 inch thick.
6. Heat a nonstick skillet over medium heat and cook each bread for 23 minutes on each side until lightly golden and puffed.
7. Serve warm with your favorite dips or fillings.

Nutritional Info: Calories: 180 | Fat: 4g | Carbs: 30g | Protein: 5g

Bread Machine Function: Dough cycle.

Indian Naan

Prep: 15 mins | Cook: 15 mins | Serves: 6 pieces

Ingredients:
- **US:** 2 cups allpurpose flour, 1 teaspoon baking powder, 1/2 teaspoon baking soda, 1/4 teaspoon salt, 2 tablespoons plain yogurt, 1 tablespoon melted butter, 1/2 cup lukewarm water

- **UK:** 250g allpurpose flour, 5g baking powder, 2.5g baking soda, 2.5g salt, 30g plain yogurt, 15g melted butter, 120ml lukewarm water

Instructions:
1. In the bread machine pan, combine lukewarm water, yogurt, and melted butter.
2. Add flour, baking powder, baking soda, and salt to the pan.
3. Select the "Dough" cycle and start the machine.
4. Once the dough is ready, divide it into 6 equal portions and roll each into an oval shape.
5. Preheat the grill to high heat.
6. Place the naan on the grill and cook for 23 minutes on each side until puffed and lightly charred.
7. Brush with melted butter before serving.

Nutritional Info: Calories: 150 | Fat: 3g | Carbs: 25g | Protein: 4g

Bread Machine Function: Dough cycle.

Mexican Bolillos

Prep: 15 mins | Cook: 20 mins | Serves: 6 bolillos

Ingredients:
- **US:** 3 cups bread flour, 1 teaspoon salt, 1 tablespoon sugar, 1 tablespoon vegetable oil, 1 tablespoon active dry yeast, 1 cup warm water
- **UK:** 375g bread flour, 5g salt, 12g sugar, 15ml vegetable oil, 7g active dry yeast, 240ml warm water

Instructions:
1. Add warm water, sugar, and yeast to the bread machine pan. Let it sit for 5 minutes until frothy.
2. Add bread flour, salt, and vegetable oil to the pan.
3. Select the "Dough" cycle and start the machine.

4. Once the dough is ready, divide it into 6 equal portions and shape each into an oval.
5. Place the dough on a baking sheet lined with parchment paper, cover, and let it rise for 30 minutes.
6. Preheat the oven to 400°F (200°C).
7. Bake the bolillos for 1520 minutes until golden brown and hollowsounding when tapped on the bottom.
8. Let them cool on a wire rack before serving.

Nutritional Info: Calories: 220 | Fat: 3g | Carbs: 40g | Protein: 7g

Bread Machine Function: Dough cycle.

Japanese Milk Bread

Prep: 15 mins | Cook: 25 mins | Serves: 1 loaf

Ingredients:
- **US:** 2 cups bread flour, 1/4 cup sugar, 1 teaspoon salt, 2 tablespoons unsalted butter, 1 egg, 1/2 cup milk, 2 teaspoons active dry yeast
- **UK:** 250g bread flour, 50g sugar, 5g salt, 30g unsalted butter, 1 egg, 120ml milk, 7g active dry yeast

Instructions:
1. Place milk, sugar, and yeast in the bread machine pan. Let it rest for 5 minutes.
2. Add bread flour, salt, butter, and egg to the pan.
3. Select the "Dough" cycle and start the machine.
4. Once the dough is ready, remove it from the machine and shape it into a loaf.
5. Place the dough in a greased loaf pan, cover, and let it rise for 3045 minutes.
6. Preheat the oven to 350°F (175°C).
7. Bake the bread for 2530 minutes until golden brown and hollowsounding when tapped on the bottom.
8. Let it cool before slicing and serving.

Nutritional Info: Calories: 200 | Fat: 5g | Carbs: 32g | Protein: 6g

Bread Machine Function: Dough cycle.

Chinese Steamed Buns

Prep: 20 mins | Cook: 15 mins | Serves: 12 buns

Ingredients:
- **US:** 2 cups allpurpose flour, 1 tablespoon sugar, 1 teaspoon salt, 1 tablespoon vegetable oil, 1 teaspoon active dry yeast, 3/4 cup lukewarm water
- **UK:** 250g allpurpose flour, 12g sugar, 5g salt, 15ml vegetable oil, 7g active dry yeast, 180ml lukewarm water

Instructions:
1. In the bread machine pan, combine lukewarm water, sugar, and yeast. Let it rest for 5 minutes.
2. Add flour, salt, and vegetable oil to the pan.
3. Select the "Dough" cycle and start the machine.
4. Once the dough is ready, divide it into 12 equal portions and roll each into a ball.
5. Flatten each ball into a circle and place a portion of your desired filling in the center.
6. Gather the edges of the dough and pinch to seal, then place each bun on a piece of parchment paper.
7. Arrange the buns in a steamer basket, cover, and let them rest for 15 minutes.
8. Steam the buns over boiling water for 1215 minutes until puffed and cooked through.

Nutritional Info: Calories: 120 | Fat: 2g | Carbs: 23g | Protein: 3g

Bread Machine Function: Dough cycle.

Swedish Limpa

Prep: 15 mins | Cook: 30 mins | Serves: 1 loaf

Ingredients:
- **US:** 1 cup rye flour, 1 cup bread flour, 1/4 cup dark corn syrup, 1 tablespoon molasses, 1 tablespoon butter, 1 teaspoon salt, 1 teaspoon caraway seeds, 1 teaspoon active dry yeast, 3/4 cup warm water
- **UK:** 125g rye flour, 125g bread flour, 60ml dark corn syrup, 15ml molasses, 15g butter, 5g salt, 5g caraway seeds, 7g active dry yeast, 180ml warm water

Instructions:
1. In the bread machine pan, combine warm water, dark corn syrup, molasses, and yeast. Let it sit for 5 minutes.
2. Add rye flour, bread flour, salt, butter, and caraway seeds to the pan.
3. Select the "Basic" or "Whole Wheat" cycle and start the machine.
4. Once the dough is ready, shape it into a loaf and place it in a greased loaf pan.
5. Cover the loaf and let it rise for 3045 minutes.
6. Preheat the oven to 375°F (190°C).
7. Bake the bread for 2530 minutes until golden brown and sounds hollow when tapped on the bottom.
8. Let it cool before slicing and serving.

Nutritional Info: Calories: 150 | Fat: 2g | Carbs: 30g | Protein: 4g

Bread Machine Function: Basic or Whole Wheat cycle.

Russian Rye Bread

Prep: 15 mins | Cook: 40 mins | Serves: 1 loaf

Ingredients:
- **US:** 1 1/2 cups rye flour, 1 1/2 cups bread flour, 1 tablespoon caraway seeds, 1 tablespoon honey, 1 tablespoon vegetable oil, 1 teaspoon salt, 1 teaspoon active dry yeast, 1 cup warm water
- **UK:** 190g rye flour, 190g bread flour, 15g caraway seeds, 15g honey, 15ml vegetable oil, 5g salt, 7g active dry yeast, 240ml warm water

Instructions:
1. Place warm water, honey, and yeast in the bread machine pan. Let it sit for 5 minutes.
2. Add rye flour, bread flour, salt, vegetable oil, and caraway seeds to the pan.
3. Select the "Basic" or "Whole Wheat" cycle and start the machine.
4. Once the dough is ready, shape it into a loaf and place it in a greased loaf pan.
5. Cover the loaf and let it rise for 3045 minutes.
6. Preheat the oven to 375°F (190°C).
7. Bake the bread for 3540 minutes until dark brown and sounds hollow when tapped on the bottom.
8. Let it cool before slicing and serving.

Nutritional Info: Calories: 160 | Fat: 2g | Carbs: 30g | Protein: 5g

Bread Machine Function: Basic or Whole Wheat cycle.

Polish Babka

Prep: 20 mins | Cook: 45 mins | Serves: 1 loaf

Ingredients:
- **US:** 3 cups allpurpose flour, 1/4 cup sugar, 1/4 cup butter (softened), 2 eggs, 1/2 cup warm milk, 1/4 cup warm water, 2 1/4 teaspoons active dry yeast, 1 teaspoon vanilla extract, 1/2 teaspoon salt, 1/4 cup raisins (optional)
- **UK:** 375g allpurpose flour, 50g sugar, 60g butter (softened), 2 eggs, 120ml warm milk, 60ml warm water, 7g active dry yeast, 5ml vanilla extract, 3g salt, 40g raisins (optional)

Instructions:
1. In the bread machine pan, combine warm milk, warm water, sugar, and yeast. Let it sit for 5 minutes.
2. Add flour, softened butter, eggs, vanilla extract, and salt to the pan.
3. Select the "Dough" cycle and start the machine.
4. Once the dough is ready, remove it from the machine and knead in raisins if desired.
5. Shape the dough into a loaf and place it in a greased loaf pan.
6. Cover the loaf and let it rise for 3045 minutes.
7. Preheat the oven to 350°F (175°C).
8. Bake the bread for 4045 minutes until golden brown and sounds hollow when tapped on the bottom.

Nutritional Info: Calories: 190 | Fat: 5g | Carbs: 30g | Protein: 6g

Bread Machine Function: Dough cycle.

Irish Soda Bread

Prep: 15 mins | Cook: 45 mins | Serves: 1 loaf

Ingredients:
- **US:** 3 cups allpurpose flour, 1 teaspoon baking soda, 1 teaspoon salt, 1 1/4 cups buttermilk
- **UK:** 375g allpurpose flour, 5g baking soda, 5g salt, 300ml buttermilk

Instructions:
1. Preheat the oven to 375°F (190°C). Grease a baking sheet or line it with parchment paper.
2. In a large bowl, whisk together the flour, baking soda, and salt.
3. Make a well in the center of the dry ingredients and pour in the buttermilk.
4. Mix until the dough comes together. It should be soft but not too sticky.
5. Shape the dough into a round loaf and place it on the prepared baking sheet.
6. Using a sharp knife, score an 'X' on the top of the loaf.
7. Bake for 4045 minutes, or until the bread is golden brown and sounds hollow when tapped on the bottom.
8. Let the bread cool on a wire rack before slicing and serving.

Nutritional Info: Calories: 160 | Fat: 0.5g | Carbs: 33g | Protein: 5g

Bread Machine Function: N/A

Portuguese Sweet Bread

Prep: 20 mins | Cook: 40 mins | Serves: 1 loaf

Ingredients:
- **US:** 3 cups bread flour, 1/4 cup sugar, 2 teaspoons active dry yeast, 1/2 teaspoon salt, 1/4 cup milk, 1/4 cup water, 1/4 cup butter (softened), 2 eggs
- **UK:** 375g bread flour, 50g sugar, 7g active dry yeast, 5g salt, 60ml milk, 60ml water, 60g butter (softened), 2 eggs

Instructions:
1. In the bread machine pan, combine warm milk, warm water, sugar, and yeast. Let it sit for 5 minutes.
2. Add bread flour, softened butter, eggs, and salt to the pan.
3. Select the "Basic" or "Sweet" cycle and start the machine.
4. Once the dough is ready, remove it from the machine and shape it into a loaf.
5. Place the dough in a greased loaf pan, cover it, and let it rise for 3045 minutes.
6. Preheat the oven to 350°F (175°C).
7. Bake the bread for 3540 minutes, or until golden brown and sounds hollow when tapped on the bottom.
8. Allow the bread to cool before slicing and serving.

Nutritional Info: Calories: 180 | Fat: 5g | Carbs: 28g | Protein: 5g

Bread Machine Function: Basic or Sweet cycle.

Cuban Bread

Prep: 15 mins | Cook: 25 mins | Serves: 1 loaf

Ingredients:
- **US:** 3 cups bread flour, 1 teaspoon salt, 1 tablespoon sugar, 2 teaspoons active dry yeast, 1 cup warm water, 1 tablespoon lard or vegetable oil
- **UK:** 375g bread flour, 5g salt, 15g sugar, 7g active dry yeast, 240ml warm water, 15ml lard or vegetable oil

Instructions:
1. In the bread machine pan, combine warm water, sugar, and yeast. Let it sit for 5 minutes.
2. Add bread flour, salt, and lard or vegetable oil to the pan.
3. Select the "Dough" cycle and start the machine.
4. Once the dough is ready, remove it from the machine and shape it into a loaf.
5. Place the dough on a baking sheet lined with parchment paper.
6. Cover the dough and let it rise for 3045 minutes.
7. Preheat the oven to 400°F (200°C).
8. Bake the bread for 2025 minutes, or until golden brown and sounds hollow when tapped on the bottom.

Nutritional Info: Calories: 150 | Fat: 2g | Carbs: 28g | Protein: 5g

Bread Machine Function: Dough cycle.

Brazilian Cheese Bread

Prep: 15 mins | Cook: 20 mins | Serves: 24 rolls

Ingredients:
- **US:** 1 cup milk, 1/2 cup vegetable oil, 2 cups tapioca flour, 1 teaspoon salt, 2 eggs, 1 1/2 cups grated Parmesan cheese

- **UK:** 240ml milk, 120ml vegetable oil, 240g tapioca flour, 5g salt, 2 eggs, 170g grated Parmesan cheese

Instructions:
1. Preheat the oven to 375°F (190°C). Grease a mini muffin tin.
2. In a saucepan, combine milk and oil. Bring to a gentle boil.
3. Remove from heat and stir in tapioca flour until smooth.
4. Allow the mixture to cool slightly, then transfer to a mixing bowl.
5. Beat in the eggs one at a time until fully incorporated.
6. Stir in the grated Parmesan cheese until well combined.
7. Spoon the batter into the prepared mini muffin tin, filling each cup almost to the top.
8. Bake for 1520 minutes until puffed up and lightly golden.

Nutritional Info: Calories: 120 | Fat: 7g | Carbs: 9g | Protein: 4g

Bread Machine Function: N/A

Moroccan Khobz

Prep: 20 mins | Cook: 25 mins | Serves: 1 loaf

Ingredients:
- **US:** 3 cups allpurpose flour, 1 tablespoon sugar, 1 teaspoon salt, 2 teaspoons active dry yeast, 1 1/4 cups warm water
- **UK:** 375g allpurpose flour, 15g sugar, 5g salt, 7g active dry yeast, 300ml warm water

Instructions:
1. In the bread machine pan, combine warm water, sugar, and yeast. Let it sit for 5 minutes.
2. Add allpurpose flour and salt to the pan.
3. Select the "Dough" cycle and start the machine.
4. Once the dough is ready, remove it from the machine and shape it into a round loaf.

5. Place the dough on a baking sheet lined with parchment paper.
6. Cover the dough and let it rise for 3045 minutes.
7. Preheat the oven to 400°F (200°C).
8. Bake the bread for 2025 minutes, or until golden brown and sounds hollow when tapped on the bottom.

Nutritional Info: Calories: 130 | Fat: 0.5g | Carbs: 27g | Protein: 4g

Bread Machine Function: Dough cycle.

Turkish Pide

Prep: 20 mins | Cook: 25 mins | Serves: 4 servings

Ingredients:

   US: 3 cups allpurpose flour, 1 tablespoon active dry yeast, 1 teaspoon sugar, 1 teaspoon salt, 1 cup warm water, 2 tablespoons olive oil

   UK: 375g allpurpose flour, 7g active dry yeast, 5g sugar, 5g salt, 240ml warm water, 30ml olive oil

Instructions:
1. In the bread machine pan, combine warm water, sugar, and yeast. Let it sit for 5 minutes until foamy.
2. Add allpurpose flour, salt, and olive oil to the pan.
3. Select the "Dough" cycle and start the machine.
4. Once the dough is ready, divide it into 4 equal portions and shape each into an oval.
5. Place the ovals on a baking sheet lined with parchment paper, cover, and let them rise for 20 minutes.
6. Preheat the oven to 425°F (220°C).
7. Using your fingers, make indentations all over the surface of each oval.
8. Bake for 1520 minutes until golden brown.

Nutritional Info: Calories: 250 | Fat: 6g | Carbs: 41g | Protein: 7g

Bread Machine Function: Dough cycle.

CHAPTER NINE: BREAD MACHINE DOUGHS

Perfect Pizza Dough

Prep: 10 mins | Cook: N/A | Serves: 2 pizza crusts

Ingredients:
- **US:** 2 cups bread flour, 1 teaspoon salt, 1 teaspoon sugar, 1 tablespoon olive oil, ¾ cup warm water, 1 packet (2 ¼ teaspoons) active dry yeast
- **UK:** 250g bread flour, 5g salt, 5g sugar, 15ml olive oil, 180ml warm water, 1 packet (7g) active dry yeast

Instructions:
1. Add warm water, sugar, and yeast to the bread machine pan. Let it sit for 5 minutes until foamy.
2. Add bread flour, salt, and olive oil to the pan.
3. Select the "Dough" cycle and start the machine.
4. Once the dough is ready, divide it into 2 equal portions and shape each into a ball.
5. Roll out each ball into a round pizza crust.
6. Add your favorite toppings and bake in a preheated oven at 475°F (245°C) for 1012 minutes, or until crust is golden and toppings are bubbly.

Nutritional Info: Calories: 250 | Fat: 4g | Carbs: 46g | Protein: 7g

Bread Machine Function: Dough cycle.

Calzone Dough

Prep: 10 mins | Cook: N/A | Serves: 2 calzones

Ingredients:
- **US:** 2 cups allpurpose flour, 1 teaspoon salt, 1 teaspoon sugar, 1 tablespoon olive oil, ¾ cup warm water, 1 packet active dry yeast
- **UK:** 250g allpurpose flour, 5g salt, 5g sugar, 15ml olive oil, 180ml warm water, 1 packet active dry yeast

Instructions:
1. In the bread machine pan, add warm water and sugar. Sprinkle yeast over the water and let it sit for 5 minutes until foamy.
2. Add allpurpose flour, salt, and olive oil to the pan.
3. Select the "Dough" cycle and start the machine.
4. Once the dough is ready, divide it into 2 equal portions.
5. Roll out each portion into a circle about 8 inches in diameter.
6. Place your desired fillings on one half of each circle, leaving a border around the edge.
7. Fold the other half of the dough over the fillings and crimp the edges to seal.
8. Bake in a preheated oven at 400°F (200°C) for 2025 minutes, or until golden brown.

Nutritional Info: (Calories will vary depending on fillings)

Bread Machine Function: Dough cycle.

Stromboli Dough

Prep: 15 mins | Cook: 20 mins | Serves: 4 strombolis

Ingredients:
- **US:** 2 cups allpurpose flour, 1 teaspoon instant yeast, 1 teaspoon sugar, 1 teaspoon salt, ¾ cup warm water, 2 tablespoons olive oil
- **UK:** 250g plain flour, 7g instant yeast, 7g sugar, 7g salt, 180ml warm water, 30ml olive oil

Instructions:
1. In the bread machine pan, combine warm water, sugar, and instant yeast. Let it sit for 5 minutes until foamy.
2. Add allpurpose flour, salt, and olive oil to the pan.
3. Select the "Dough" cycle and start the machine.
4. Once the dough is ready, divide it into 4 equal portions.
5. Roll out each portion into a rectangle shape, about 1/4 inch thick.
6. Place desired fillings (such as cooked Italian sausage, pepperoni, bell peppers, onions, and mozzarella cheese) evenly over the dough, leaving a border around the edges.
7. Roll up each rectangle tightly, starting from the long side, to form a log shape.
8. Place the strombolis seam side down on a baking sheet lined with parchment paper.
9. Make a few slits on top of each stromboli to allow steam to escape.
10. Brush the tops of the strombolis with olive oil.
11. Bake in a preheated oven at 400°F (200°C) for 2025 minutes, or until golden brown.

Bread Machine Function: Dough cycle.

Classic Cinnamon Roll Dough

Prep: 15 mins | Cook: N/A | Serves: 12 cinnamon rolls

Ingredients:
- **US:** 3 ½ cups allpurpose flour, ¼ cup granulated sugar, 1 teaspoon salt, 1 cup warm milk, 2 eggs, ¼ cup unsalted butter, 2 ¼ teaspoons active dry yeast
- **UK:** 440g allpurpose flour, 50g granulated sugar, 5g salt, 240ml warm milk, 2 eggs, 60g unsalted butter, 1 packet (7g) active dry yeast

Instructions:
1. In the bread machine pan, combine warm milk, sugar, and yeast. Let it sit for 5 minutes until frothy.
2. Add eggs, melted butter, salt, and flour to the pan.
3. Select the "Dough" cycle and start the machine.
4. Once the dough is ready, roll it out into a rectangle on a floured surface.
5. Spread cinnamonsugar mixture evenly over the dough, then roll it up tightly.
6. Cut the roll into 12 equal pieces and place them in a greased baking dish.
7. Let the rolls rise for 30 minutes, then bake in a preheated oven at 375°F (190°C) for 2025 minutes, or until golden brown.

Nutritional Info: Calories: 220 | Fat: 7g | Carbs: 35g | Protein: 5g

Bread Machine Function: Dough cycle.

Pretzel Dough

Prep: 15 mins | Cook: 15 mins | Serves: 8 pretzels

Ingredients:
   US: 2 cups allpurpose flour, 1 tablespoon sugar, 1 teaspoon salt, 1 cup warm water, 2 ¼ teaspoons active dry yeast, 2 tablespoons baking soda, 1 egg (beaten), coarse salt for topping

   UK: 250g allpurpose flour, 15g sugar, 5g salt, 240ml warm water, 1 packet active dry yeast, 30g baking soda, 1 egg (beaten), coarse salt for topping

Instructions:
1. In the bread machine pan, add warm water and sugar. Sprinkle yeast over the water and let it sit for 5 minutes until foamy.
2. Add allpurpose flour and salt to the pan.
3. Select the "Dough" cycle and start the machine.
4. Once the dough is ready, divide it into 8 equal portions.
5. Roll each portion into a rope about 18 inches long.
6. Shape each rope into a pretzel shape.
7. In a large pot, bring water and baking soda to a boil.
8. Boil each pretzel for 30 seconds, then remove with a slotted spoon and place on a baking sheet lined with parchment paper.
9. Brush each pretzel with beaten egg and sprinkle with coarse salt.
10. Bake in a preheated oven at 425°F (220°C) for 1215 minutes, or until golden brown.

Nutritional Info: Calories: 150 | Fat: 1g | Carbs: 30g | Protein: 5g

Bread Machine Function: Dough cycle.

Homemade Bagel Dough

Prep: 15 mins | Cook: N/A | Serves: 8 bagels

Ingredients:
- **US:** 3 ½ cups bread flour, 1 ½ teaspoons salt, 1 tablespoon granulated sugar, 1 cup warm water, 2 ¼ teaspoons active dry yeast
- **UK:** 440g bread flour, 7g salt, 15g granulated sugar, 240ml warm water, 1 packet (7g) active dry yeast

Instructions:
1. Combine warm water, sugar, and yeast in the bread machine pan. Let it sit for 5 minutes until foamy.
2. Add bread flour and salt to the pan.
3. Select the "Dough" cycle and start the machine.
4. Once the dough is ready, divide it into 8 equal portions and shape each into a ball.
5. Flatten each ball and poke a hole in the center to form a bagel shape.
6. Let the bagels rest for 20 minutes, then bring a large pot of water to a boil.
7. Boil each bagel for 12 minutes on each side, then place them on a baking sheet.
8. Bake in a preheated oven at 425°F (220°C) for 2025 minutes, or until golden brown.

Nutritional Info: Calories: 200 | Fat: 1g | Carbs: 40g | Protein: 7g

Bread Machine Function: Dough cycle.

English Muffin Dough

Prep: 10 mins | Cook: N/A | Serves: 12 English muffins

Ingredients:
- **US:** 3 cups allpurpose flour, 1 cup milk, 1 tablespoon granulated sugar, 1 teaspoon salt, 2 tablespoons unsalted butter, 1 packet (2 ¼ teaspoons) active dry yeast, Cornmeal for dusting
- **UK:** 375g allpurpose flour, 240ml milk, 15g granulated sugar, 5g salt, 30g unsalted butter, 1 packet (7g) active dry yeast, Cornmeal for dusting

Instructions:
1. Warm milk and melt butter together in a small saucepan until butter is just melted. Let it cool slightly.
2. In the bread machine pan, combine warm milk mixture, sugar, and yeast. Let it sit for 5 minutes until foamy.
3. Add flour and salt to the pan.
4. Select the "Dough" cycle and start the machine.
5. Once the dough is ready, roll it out on a floured surface to about ½ inch thick.
6. Use a round cutter to cut out muffins. Dust each with cornmeal and place on a baking sheet.
7. Let them rise for 2030 minutes.
8. Cook on a lightly greased griddle over medium heat for about 10 minutes on each side, or until golden brown and cooked through.

Nutritional Info: Calories: 150 | Fat: 2g | Carbs: 28g | Protein: 4g

Bread Machine Function: Dough cycle.

Buttery Croissant Dough

Prep: 20 mins | Cook: N/A | Serves: 12 croissants

Ingredients:
- **US:** 2 cups allpurpose flour, 1 tablespoon granulated sugar, 1 teaspoon salt, 1 tablespoon active dry yeast, ½ cup warm milk, ½ cup unsalted butter (cold, cut into small pieces), 1 egg (beaten), Butter for laminating
- **UK:** 250g allpurpose flour, 15g granulated sugar, 5g salt, 7g active dry yeast, 120ml warm milk, 115g unsalted butter (cold, cut into small pieces), 1 egg (beaten), Butter for laminating

Instructions:
1. Combine warm milk and yeast in the bread machine pan. Let it sit for 5 minutes until foamy.
2. Add flour, sugar, salt, and cold butter to the pan.
3. Select the "Dough" cycle and start the machine.
4. Once the dough is ready, roll it out on a floured surface into a rectangle.
5. Spread softened butter over 2/3 of the dough, then fold the unbuttered third over the middle, followed by the remaining third.
6. Roll out the dough again and repeat the folding process.
7. Wrap the dough in plastic wrap and chill in the refrigerator for at least 1 hour or overnight.
8. Roll out the chilled dough, cut into triangles, and roll each triangle into a croissant shape.
9. Place the croissants on a baking sheet lined with parchment paper, cover, and let rise for 12 hours.
10. Preheat the oven to 375°F (190°C).
11. Brush the croissants with beaten egg and bake for 1520 minutes, or until golden brown and flaky.

Nutritional Info: Calories: 180 | Fat: 10g | Carbs: 19g | Protein: 4g

Bread Machine Function: Dough cycle.

Danish Dough

Prep: 15 mins | Cook: N/A | Serves: 12 pastries

Ingredients:
- **US:** 2 cups allpurpose flour, ¼ cup granulated sugar, ½ teaspoon salt, 1 packet (2 ¼ teaspoons) active dry yeast, ⅓ cup warm milk, 2 eggs, ½ cup unsalted butter (softened)
- **UK:** 250g allpurpose flour, 50g granulated sugar, 5g salt, 1 packet (7g) active dry yeast, 80ml warm milk, 2 eggs, 115g unsalted butter (softened)

Instructions:
1. In the bread machine pan, combine warm milk, sugar, and yeast. Let it sit for 5 minutes until frothy.
2. Add flour, salt, eggs, and softened butter to the pan.
3. Select the "Dough" cycle and start the machine.
4. Once the dough is ready, roll it out on a floured surface into a rectangle.
5. Fold the dough into thirds like a letter, then roll it out again into a rectangle.
6. Repeat the folding process twice more, then wrap the dough in plastic wrap and refrigerate for at least 1 hour.
7. Roll out the chilled dough and cut into squares.
8. Place a dollop of your favorite filling (such as fruit preserves or pastry cream) in the center of each square.
9. Fold the corners of the square over the filling and pinch to seal.
10. Place the pastries on a baking sheet lined with parchment paper, cover, and let rise for 30 minutes.
11. Preheat the oven to 375°F (190°C) and bake for 1520 minutes, or until golden brown.

Nutritional Info: Calories: 200 | Fat: 8g | Carbs: 28g | Protein: 4g

Bread Machine Function: Dough cycle.

Puff Pastry Dough

Prep: 15 mins | Cook: N/A | Serves: 1 pastry sheet

Ingredients:
- **US:** 2 cups allpurpose flour, 1 teaspoon salt, 1 cup unsalted butter (chilled, cut into cubes), ½ cup cold water
- **UK:** 250g allpurpose flour, 5g salt, 225g unsalted butter (chilled, cut into cubes), 120ml cold water

Instructions:
1. In the bread machine pan, combine flour and salt.
2. Add chilled butter cubes to the pan and pulse in the bread machine until the mixture resembles coarse crumbs.
3. Slowly add cold water while pulsing until the dough comes together.
4. Remove the dough from the bread machine and shape it into a rectangle.
5. Wrap the dough in plastic wrap and refrigerate for 30 minutes.
6. Roll out the chilled dough on a floured surface into a rectangle.
7. Fold the dough into thirds like a letter, then rotate it 90 degrees and roll it out again into a rectangle.
8. Repeat the folding process twice more, then wrap the dough in plastic wrap and refrigerate for at least 1 hour.
9. Use the puff pastry dough as desired for sweet or savory pastries.

Nutritional Info: Calories: 180 | Fat: 12g | Carbs: 15g | Protein: 2g

Bread Machine Function: Pulse function.

Pie Crust Dough

Prep: 10 mins | Cook: N/A | Serves: 1 pie crust

Ingredients:
- **US:** 1 ¼ cups allpurpose flour, ½ teaspoon salt, ½ cup unsalted butter (cold, cut into cubes), 23 tablespoons ice water
- **UK:** 155g allpurpose flour, 2.5g salt, 115g unsalted butter (cold, cut into cubes), 3045ml ice water

Instructions:
1. In the bread machine pan, combine flour and salt.
2. Add chilled butter cubes to the pan and pulse in the bread machine until the mixture resembles coarse crumbs.
3. Slowly add ice water while pulsing until the dough comes together.
4. Remove the dough from the bread machine and shape it into a ball.
5. Flatten the dough into a disk, wrap it in plastic wrap, and refrigerate for at least 30 minutes.
6. Roll out the chilled dough on a floured surface into a circle large enough to fit your pie dish.
7. Gently transfer the dough to the pie dish and trim any excess around the edges.
8. Fill and bake the pie according to your recipe.

Nutritional Info: Calories: 150 | Fat: 10g | Carbs: 13g | Protein: 2g

Bread Machine Function: Pulse function.

Breadstick Dough

Prep: 10 mins | Cook: N/A | Serves: 12 breadsticks

Ingredients:
- **US:** 2 cups bread flour, 1 teaspoon salt, 1 tablespoon granulated sugar, 1 tablespoon olive oil, ¾ cup warm water, 1 packet (2 ¼ teaspoons) active dry yeast
- **UK:** 250g bread flour, 5g salt, 15g granulated sugar, 15ml olive oil, 180ml warm water, 1 packet (7g) active dry yeast

Instructions:
1. In the bread machine pan, combine warm water, sugar, and yeast. Let it sit for 5 minutes until frothy.
2. Add bread flour, salt, and olive oil to the pan.
3. Select the "Dough" cycle and start the machine.
4. Once the dough is ready, divide it into 12 equal portions and roll each into a breadstick shape.
5. Place the breadsticks on a baking sheet lined with parchment paper, cover, and let rise for 30 minutes.
6. Preheat the oven to 375°F (190°C).
7. Bake the breadsticks for 1215 minutes, or until golden brown.
8. Serve warm with your favorite dipping sauce.

Nutritional Info: Calories: 120 | Fat: 1g | Carbs: 23g | Protein: 4g

Bread Machine Function: Dough cycle.

Tortilla Dough

Prep: 10 mins | Cook: N/A | Serves: 12 tortillas

Ingredients:
- **US:** 2 cups allpurpose flour, ½ teaspoon salt, 1 tablespoon vegetable oil, ¾ cup warm water

- **UK:** 250g allpurpose flour, 5g salt, 15ml vegetable oil, 180ml warm water

Instructions:
1. In the bread machine pan, combine flour and salt.
2. Add vegetable oil and warm water to the pan.
3. Select the "Dough" cycle and start the machine.
4. Once the dough is ready, divide it into 12 equal portions and roll each into a ball.
5. Flatten each ball with a rolling pin into a thin circle.
6. Heat a nonstick skillet over mediumhigh heat.
7. Cook each tortilla for about 30 seconds on each side, or until lightly browned and puffy.
8. Keep warm in a clean kitchen towel while cooking the remaining tortillas.

Nutritional Info: Calories: 90 | Fat: 1g | Carbs: 17g | Protein: 2g

Bread Machine Function: Dough cycle.

Naan Dough

Prep: 15 mins | Cook: N/A | Serves: 8 naan breads

Ingredients:
- **US:** 2 cups allpurpose flour, 1 teaspoon sugar, 1 teaspoon salt, 1 teaspoon baking powder, 2 tablespoons plain yogurt, 2 tablespoons vegetable oil, ¾ cup warm milk
- **UK:** 250g allpurpose flour, 5g sugar, 5g salt, 5g baking powder, 30g plain yogurt, 30ml vegetable oil, 180ml warm milk

Instructions:
1. In the bread machine pan, combine flour, sugar, salt, and baking powder.
2. Add plain yogurt, vegetable oil, and warm milk to the pan.
3. Select the "Dough" cycle and start the machine.

4. Once the dough is ready, divide it into 8 equal portions and roll each into a ball.
5. Roll out each ball into a circle about ¼ inch thick.
6. Heat a skillet or griddle over mediumhigh heat.
7. Cook each naan for about 12 minutes on each side, or until lightly browned and bubbly.
8. Brush with melted butter and serve warm.

Nutritional Info: Calories: 160 | Fat: 4g | Carbs: 27g | Protein: 5g

Bread Machine Function: Dough cycle.

Pita Dough

Prep: 15 mins | Cook: N/A | Serves: 8 pitas

Ingredients:
- **US:** 2 cups bread flour, 1 teaspoon salt, 1 tablespoon granulated sugar, 1 tablespoon olive oil, 1 cup warm water, 1 packet (2 ¼ teaspoons) active dry yeast
- **UK:** 250g bread flour, 5g salt, 15g granulated sugar, 15ml olive oil, 240ml warm water, 1 packet (7g) active dry yeast

Instructions:
1. In the bread machine pan, combine warm water, sugar, and yeast. Let it sit for 5 minutes until frothy.
2. Add bread flour, salt, and olive oil to the pan.
3. Select the "Dough" cycle and start the machine.
4. Once the dough is ready, divide it into 8 equal portions and roll each into a ball.
5. Roll out each ball into a circle about ¼ inch thick.
6. Preheat the oven to 475°F (245°C) with a baking stone or overturned baking sheet inside.
7. Place the rolledout pitas directly onto the hot baking surface and bake for 34 minutes, or until puffed and lightly browned.
8. Remove from the oven and let cool slightly before serving.

Nutritional Info: Calories: 150 | Fat: 2g | Carbs: 28g | Protein: 5g

Bread Machine Function: Dough cycle.

Flatbread Dough

Prep: 10 mins | Cook: N/A | Serves: 8 flatbreads

Ingredients:
- **US:** 2 cups allpurpose flour, 1 teaspoon salt, 1 tablespoon olive oil, ¾ cup warm water, 1 packet (2 ¼ teaspoons) active dry yeast
- **UK:** 250g allpurpose flour, 5g salt, 15ml olive oil, 180ml warm water, 1 packet (7g) active dry yeast

Instructions:
1. In the bread machine pan, combine warm water and yeast. Let it sit for 5 minutes until frothy.
2. Add allpurpose flour, salt, and olive oil to the pan.
3. Select the "Dough" cycle and start the machine.
4. Once the dough is ready, divide it into 8 equal portions and roll each into a ball.
5. Roll out each ball into a circle about ¼ inch thick.
6. Heat a skillet or griddle over mediumhigh heat.
7. Cook each flatbread for about 12 minutes on each side, or until lightly browned and bubbly.
8. Serve warm with your favorite toppings or fillings.

Nutritional Info: Calories: 120 | Fat: 2g | Carbs: 22g | Protein: 4g

Bread Machine Function: Dough cycle.

Donut Dough

Prep: 15 mins | Cook: N/A | Serves: 12 donuts

Ingredients:
- **US:** 2 cups allpurpose flour, ½ cup granulated sugar, 1 teaspoon salt, 1 packet (2 ¼ teaspoons) active dry yeast, ¾ cup warm milk, 2 tablespoons unsalted butter (softened), 2 egg yolks, 1 teaspoon vanilla extract
- **UK:** 250g allpurpose flour, 100g granulated sugar, 5g salt, 1 packet (7g) active dry yeast, 180ml warm milk, 30g unsalted butter (softened), 2 egg yolks, 5ml vanilla extract

Instructions:
1. In the bread machine pan, combine warm milk, sugar, and yeast. Let it sit for 5 minutes until frothy.
2. Add allpurpose flour, salt, softened butter, egg yolks, and vanilla extract to the pan.
3. Select the "Dough" cycle and start the machine.
4. Once the dough is ready, roll it out on a floured surface to ½ inch thickness.
5. Use a donut cutter to cut out donut shapes, then transfer them to a baking sheet lined with parchment paper.
6. Cover the donuts and let them rise in a warm place for 3045 minutes.
7. Preheat the oil in a deep fryer or large pot to 375°F (190°C).
8. Carefully place the risen donuts into the hot oil and fry for 12 minutes on each side, or until golden brown.
9. Remove the donuts from the oil and drain on paper towels.
10. Allow them to cool slightly before glazing or topping as desired.

Nutritional Info: Calories: 180 | Fat: 5g | Carbs: 30g | Protein: 4g

Bread Machine Function: Dough cycle.

Fritter Dough

Prep: 15 mins | Cook: N/A | Serves: 12 fritters

Ingredients:
- **US:** 2 cups allpurpose flour, ½ cup granulated sugar, 1 teaspoon baking powder, ½ teaspoon salt, 1 packet (2 ¼ teaspoons) active dry yeast, ¾ cup warm milk, 2 tablespoons unsalted butter (melted), 2 eggs, 1 teaspoon vanilla extract, 1 cup diced apples (peeled and cored)
- **UK:** 250g allpurpose flour, 100g granulated sugar, 5g baking powder, 5g salt, 1 packet (7g) active dry yeast, 180ml warm milk, 30g unsalted butter (melted), 2 eggs, 5ml vanilla extract, 150g diced apples (peeled and cored)

Instructions:
1. In the bread machine pan, combine warm milk, sugar, and yeast. Let it sit for 5 minutes until frothy.
2. Add allpurpose flour, baking powder, salt, melted butter, eggs, and vanilla extract to the pan.
3. Select the "Dough" cycle and start the machine.
4. Once the dough is ready, gently fold in the diced apples until evenly distributed.
5. Heat oil in a deep fryer or large pot to 350°F (175°C).
6. Drop spoonfuls of the dough into the hot oil and fry for 34 minutes, or until golden brown and cooked through.
7. Remove the fritters from the oil and drain on paper towels.
8. Dust with powdered sugar or drizzle with glaze before serving.

Nutritional Info: Calories: 180 | Fat: 5g | Carbs: 30g | Protein: 4g

Bread Machine Function: Dough cycle.

Conclusion

With your newfound bread machine skills and the wealth of recipes, tips and tricks contained in this book, a whole new world of possibilities has opened up for you in the kitchen. Making delicious homemade bread is now just a few simple steps away whenever you have a craving for that indescribably comforting aroma and taste.

As you've learned, there is an astounding variety of breads you can create from the convenience of your bread maker from classic lean loaves to enriched sweet breads, from crusty rustic artisan styles to soft rolls and flatbreads influenced by cultures around the globe. Don't be afraid to experiment and make these recipes your own by tinkering with ingredients or embracing the creativity of adding fresh herbs, dried fruits, nuts, cheeses and more.

Your bread machine is more than just an appliance. It's a powerful tool for nourishing your family with highquality homemade bread, saving money compared to expensive bakery loaves, and celebrating your culinary heritage or embracing new global flavors. There's just something profoundly satisfying about the simple act of measuring flour, proofing yeast, adding the fresh ingredients, and watching as your bread maker knits it all together into a fragrant, perfectlybaked loaf.

Perhaps you were initially drawn to bread machine baking by the lure of that unmistakable aroma of freshlybaked bread wafting from the kitchen a scent deeply rooted in treasured childhood memories. Or maybe the convenience of having fresh loaves on demand, without the laborious process of handkneading and monitoring rise times, appealed to your busy modern lifestyle. Your motivations don't really matter now. What matters is that you've embarked on a journey that will create lasting memories while connecting you to the rich traditions of baking passed down through generations.

Think about it with each loaf you make, you are participating in one of the oldest yet still globallyrelevant culinary arts. The practice of combining fundamental ingredients like flour, water, salt and leavening to produce life's simple staff has existed for thousands of years across virtually every culture and civilization. There's something beautifully human about this process and the way it brings people together over shared aromas, textures, flavors and memories. Your greatgrandparents' generations may have used woodfired ovens or labored over handkneading, but their spirit is still captured when you mix up a batch of dough in your bread machine's automatic cycle.

So embrace the joy of homemade bread baking and all the marvelous experimentation that lies ahead. Imagine the pride of presenting loved ones with an impressive freshlybaked loaf of your own creation a delightfully crispyetchewy crust giving way to an aromatic, tender crumb bursting with flavor. Of course, you'll inevitably stumble upon the occasional flop along the way, but even those will become learning experiences and spark new creative inspiration.

More than just a functional kitchen appliance, your bread machine is now a creative outlet, a connection to your heritage, a way to make lasting memories with your family, a source of comfort and ultimately, a recipe for happiness. So keep that intoxicating bakery aroma alive and let your breadmaking journey continue to rise to new culinary heights!

Printed in Great Britain
by Amazon